Avionics:
Systems and Troubleshooting

A Practical Guide to Advanced Avionics *Second Edition*

Student Workbook

T.K. Eismin

Production Staff

Designer/Photographer Dustin Blyer
Production Manager Holly Bonos
Senior Designer Roberta Byerly
Designer/Lead Illustrator Amy Siever

International Standard Book Number 1-933189-22-3
ISBN 13: 978-1-933189-22-2
Order # T-AVSAT-0202

For Sale by: Avotek
A Select Aerospace Industries, Inc. company

Mail to:
P.O. Box 219
Weyers Cave, Virginia 24486
USA

Ship to:
200 Packaging Drive
Weyers Cave, Virginia 24486
USA

Toll Free: 1-800-828-6835
Telephone: 1-540-234-9090
Fax: 1-540-234-9399

Second Edition
Third Printing
Printed in the USA

www.avotek.com

Contents

To the Student

This Student Workbook was written for use with the *Avionics: Systems and Troubleshooting, A practical guide to advanced avionics* textbook by T.K. Eismin.

The Study Workbook contains three different types of questions: fill-in-the-blank, multiple-choice, and analysis. The questions are arranged by chapter and are printed on perforated pages for easy removal. The answers for each set of questions are available from your course instructor.

Fill-in-the-Blank Questions

These questions are designed to help you understand the terminologies and basic facts of the material presented in each chapter.

Multiple Choice Questions

These offer you a chance to test your knowledge of each chapter in a test-type format.

Analysis Questions

These are complex questions requiring you to access information presented in the text, analyze the data, and record your response. Successful completion of the analysis questions demonstrates that you have an understanding of the material contained in each chapter.

Chapter 1: Technical Publications and Data Management

FILL IN THE BLANK QUESTIONS

name:

date:

1. On many light and corporate type aircraft, wiring schematics are often contained in the aircraft's ________________ manual.

2. The most commonly used standard for aircraft reference materials has been established by the ________________________ .

3. The Air Transport Association (ATA) has developed a standard for the organization of technical data called ________________________ .

4. The ____ has developed a standard for the organization of aircraft publications called GAMA Specification 2.

5. According to ATA iSpecification 2200, ____________________ are used to further categorize a given chapter-section-subject of the maintenance manual.

6. When receiving updates for manuals, temporary revisions are printed on ______________ colored paper.

7. ________________ revisions are used for items that require change before the regularly scheduled revisions.

8. The ________________ of a given maintenance page is used to determine if your aircraft is covered by the information stated in that section (page) of the manual.

9. Whenever using any manual, pay particular attention to any ________________ and warnings for information to make the job safer and easier.

10. A ________________ calls attention to any methods, materials, or procedures that must be followed to avoid injury or death.

11. Considering Boeing maintenance manuals, the term ____________ listed for effectivity indicates that page applies to all aircraft covered by that series of manuals.

12. The procedures and practices used repeatedly during aircraft maintenance, troubleshooting, and repairs are contained in the ____________________ chapter of each manual.

13. A technician who wants to find a procedure used repeatedly during B-737 maintenance would look in chapter ____________ of the maintenance manual.

14. Aircraft maintenance manuals provide specific information for hangar and ____________________ maintenance activities.

15. Virtually all transport category and many complex light aircraft manufacturers follow ATA specification number ____________ when designing the wiring manual.

16. There are three broad categories of wiring manuals: 1. schematics, 2. diagrams, and ________________ .

Chapter 1: Technical Publications and Data Management

FILL IN THE BLANK QUESTIONS

name:

date:

17. ____________________ diagrams are general in nature and used to gain a general understanding of an electrical system.

18. A ____________________ schematic is typically more detailed than a simplified schematic.

19. The ________________________ list contains detailed information on wire size, types and lengths.

20. ____________________ are used to depict specific component or wire locations in the aircraft or on a subsystem, such as pins or sockets of a connector plug.

21. The wiring diagram manuals for Airbus Industrie aircraft are divided into three categories: Aircraft Schematic Manuals (ASM), Aircraft Wiring Manuals (AWM), and ______________________________.

22. The Functional Item Number (FIN) is a unique number given to each ______________________________ on the Airbus aircraft.

23. The fastest way to identify any part of the Airbus A-320 is to use the ____________________ Identification Number.

24. All aircraft wires ____________________ inches or longer must be labeled with a wire identification number.

25. ____________________ wires are considered critical to flight safety and must not be modified without specific manufacturers approval.

26. On the A-320 fly-by-wire systems, wires critical to flight safety that cannot be modified without the manufactures approval are called ____________________ wires.

27. Two common specialty wires include: shielded cable and ________________________.

28. The ____________________ diagram of a component is the diagram where that component is shown in full detail.

29. The ________________________ is a vertical plane that divides the aircraft front to rear through the center of the fuselage.

30. All aircraft have a horizontal reference called the ____________________.

31. The ________________________ is an imaginary horizontal plane that runs the length of the aircraft from nose to tail.

32. The ___________________________________ is an abbreviated maintenance manual designed specifically for line maintenance and minor troubleshooting.

Chapter 1: Technical Publications and Data Management

FILL IN THE BLANK QUESTIONS

name:

date:

33. Aircraft ______________________ are designed specifically for system troubleshooting.

34. ______________________ are used to indicate locations longitudinally along the aircraft fuselage.

35. Aircraft ______________________ are assigned to various regions of the aircraft specifically to aid in component location.

36. The ______________________ list contains information on various electrical/electronic components and references the appropriate ASM.

37. The ______________________ list contains information on specific wire connections to plugs and receptacles, terminal blocks, splices, and ground points.

38. Maintenance databases for technical documents on modern aircraft such as the Boeing 787 are often maintained directly by the ______________________.

39. The ______________________ is a part of the aircraft maintenance manual documents that contain various repair strategies for given faults.

40. Boeing Aircraft Company's ______________________ system is an example of an OEM-managed technical data.

41. The Maintenance Hangar of the Future will have maintenance databases that will produce ______________________ to be worked and signed off completely electronically (paperless maintenance).

Chapter 1: Technical Publications and Data Management

MULTIPLE CHOICE QUESTIONS

name:

date:

1. Which of the following established the General Aviation Maintenance Manual Specification 2?
   a. GAMA
   b. PAMA
   c. FAA
   d. ATA

2. Aircraft reference materials are typically written following the format established by which organization?
   a. Air Transport Association (ATA)
   b. Federal Aviation Administration (FAA)
   c. Federal Communication Commission (FCC)
   d. Boeing Commercial Airplane Company

3. In the ATA code 23-20-00, what does the "20" stand for? (Refer to Figure 1-2-1)
   a. NAV1/NAV2
   b. Transponders
   c. COM1/COM2
   d. VHF or UHF

4. The ATA iSpecification 2200 System standardizes technical data using three two-digit numbers. The first digits represent ______________, the second represent ______________, and the third represent ______________.
   a. Chapter, system, component location
   b. Chapter, aircraft type, component location
   c. Manufacturer, aircraft type, system
   d. Chapter, section, detailed information

5. According to ATA iSpecification 2200 what chapter contain communication systems?
   a. 12
   b. 23
   c. 24
   d. 34

6. According to ATA iSpecification 2200, which chapters contain airframe systems information?
   a. 1-4
   b. 5-12
   c. 12-19
   d. 20-49

7. Which of the following draws attention to any methods, materials, or procedures that must be followed to avoid injury or death?
   a. Caution
   b. Note
   c. Advisory
   d. Warning

8. What procedure found in an aircraft maintenance manual will make a task easier to perform?
   a. Caution
   b. Note
   c. Advisory
   d. Warning

9. Aircraft maintenance standard practices are typically contained in which ATA chapter?
   a. 10
   b. 20
   c. 30
   d. 40

10. In which ATA chapter of the maintenance manuals would you most likely find the procedures for installation of a contact pin into an electrical connector?
    a. 20
    b. 22
    c. 32
    d. 40

Chapter 1: Technical Publications and Data Management

MULTIPLE CHOICE QUESTIONS

name:

date:

11. Which of the following is used to provide a general understanding of a given system?
    a. Wiring diagram
    b. System schematic
    c. Wire list
    d. Block Diagram

12. According to ATA iSpecification 2200, which page block group deals with troubleshooting of various systems?
    a. 101-199
    b. 201-299
    c. 301-399
    d. 401-499

13. The Functional Identification Number (FIN) is used by which manufacturer to help technicians identify specific parts?
    a. Boeing
    b. Honeywell
    c. Airbus
    d. Cessna

14. What characteristic of an aircraft wire requires it to be labeled?
    a. All primary flight system wires
    b. All wires 3 inches or longer
    c. Life limited wires 2 inches or longer
    d. All wire critical to flight safety

15. Which diagram of a component will always show that component in the most detail?
    a. Block diagram
    b. System diagram
    c. Schematic diagram
    d. Home diagram

16. On the A-320 aircraft, when work is performed on a sensitive wire, whose signature is required for a return to service authorization?
    a. Inspector
    b. FAA member
    c. Engineer
    d. Chief pilot

17. According to ATA iSpecification 2200 what diagram shows a component in full?
    a. Block diagram
    b. Wiring diagram
    c. Home diagram
    d. Schematic diagram

18. Which of the following is an imaginary vertical plane located near the front of the aircraft which is used as a reference for aircraft measurements?
    a. The datum
    b. The water line
    c. The butt line
    d. A fuselage station

19. According to Figure 1-3-5, the pilot's EFIS displays are located in what zone of the aircraft?
    a. 245
    b. 247
    c. 248
    d. 254

20. The left wing of the aircraft is located in which of the following zones?
    a. 200
    b. 300
    c. 400
    d. 500

Chapter 1:
Technical Publications and Data Management

ANALYSIS QUESTIONS

name:

date:

1. According to Figure 1-2-4, relay R7687 will be energized during the ________________ operational phase of the APU. This will cause the relay contact to connect A2 to ________________ (A1 or A3?). The ________________ note indicates when relay R7687 is energized. Is relay R7687 shown in its home diagram, yes or no?

2. Refer to Figure 1-2-12A and specify which wires are connected to the following if the A1R line contactor relay is energized. (Note: A1R is located in the top right portion of Figure 1-2-12A.)

   a. wire # J1-2-K1-12 connects to wire # ____________

   b. wire # J1-5-K1-22 connects to wire # ____________

3. Refer to Figures 1-2-12 (A and B), 1-3-4 and 1-3-5 to answer the following questions concerning the R DC POWER PANEL ASSY A3 located in the top right section of Figure 1-2-12A:

   a. What is the complete code and reference number for that assembly? ____________

   b. Record the part number for the assembly. ____________

   c. In which zone is the assembly located? ____________

   d. Give a general description where that assembly can be found on the aircraft. ____________

   ____

4. Refer to Figures 1-2-12 (A and B), 1-3-4 and 1-3-5 to answer the following questions concerning the Generator Reset Circuit Breaker located in the left center section of Figure 1-2-12A:

   a. What is the complete code and reference number for the Circuit Breaker (CB)? ____________

   b. Record the part number for the CB. ____________

   c. Record the zone where the CB is located. ____________

   d. Give a general description where the CB can be found on the aircraft. ____________

   ____

Chapter 1: Technical Publications and Data Management

ANALYSIS QUESTIONS

name:

date:

5. Decipher the transport category wire code W563-NJ299-18B using Figure 1-2-18. Show which letters/numbers correspond to the different aspects of the wire code.

   a. Wire bundle location: __________

   b. Wire system function: __________

   c. Wire number: __________

   d. Wire gauge: __________

   e. Wire color: __________

6. According to Figure 1-3-2, the forward portion of the aircraft radome is located at fuselage station __________. The leading edge of the wing root is located approximately at fuselage station __________. The trailing edge of the wing tip is located approximately at fuselage station __________. The Center of the main landing gear axle. is located approximately at fuselage station __________. (Insert numbers.)

7. Using Figure 1-3-4 determine and record the general location and wing station number for zone 550.

   a. General location: __________

   b. Out board of Wing station: __________

8. Refer to Figures 1-3-4 through 1-3-6 to answer the following questions concerning the No. 1 Inverter Power Select Relay located in the lower left side of Figure 1-3-6B:

   a. What is the complete code and reference designator (number) for the power select relay? __________

   b. Record the part number for the inverter power select relay. __________

   c. Record the zone where the inverter power select relay is located. __________

   d. Give a general description where the inverter power select relay can be found on the aircraft. __________

9. Refer to Figures 1-3-4 through 1-3-6 to answer the following questions concerning the inverter select switch located in the center of Figure 1-3-6B:

   a. What is the complete code and reference number for the inverter select switch? __________

   b. Record the part number for the switch. __________

   c. In which zone is the switch located? __________

   d. Give a general description where the switch can be found on the aircraft. __________

   ____

Chapter 1: Technical Publications and Data Management

ANALYSIS QUESTIONS

name:

date:

10. According to the diagrams in Figures 1-3-9A and B, the No. 1 generator feeder cable can be found in the ____________ (left or right?) side of the aircraft.
    Fly-by-wire (sensitive) wiring is routed through:
    Circle all that apply:

front edge left wing	trailing edge right wing
trailing edge left wing	right engine nacelle
front edge right wing	left engine nacelle

11. According to Figures 1-3-12 and 1-3-13, give the panel number and general location of the standby power circuit breaker C507.
    a. Panel number: ____________
    b. General location: ____________

12. Using Figure 1-3-13 give a general description of the location and brief description of the P126 panel on the Boeing 747-400.
    a. Panel description (name): ____________
    b. General location: ____________

13. According to Figure 1-3-15, the Center Main Equipment Center is located at station number ____________. This equipment center can be found ____________ (aft or forward?) of the flight deck and ____________ (aft or forward?) of the nose wheel strut.

14. According to Figures 1-3-11 and 1-3-15, record the following for the diode assembly R965, Opt 1:
    a. Diode part number ____________
    b. Located at panel number ____________
    c. Diagram ____________
    d. Station where part is located ____________
    e. Panel name ____________
    f. This component is located ____________ (aft or forward?) of the wing leading edge.

Chapter 1: Technical Publications and Data Management

ANALYSIS QUESTIONS

name:

date:

15. Using the diagram of the B-747-400 below, write the name of each antenna on the blank next to its corresponding number.

1. ____________________
2. ____________________
3. ____________________
4. ____________________
5. ____________________
6. ____________________
7. ____________________
8. ____________________
9. ____________________
10. ____________________
11. ____________________
12. ____________________
13. ____________________
14. ____________________
15. ____________________
16. ____________________
17. ____________________
18. ____________________
19. ____________________
20. ____________________
21. ____________________
22. ____________________

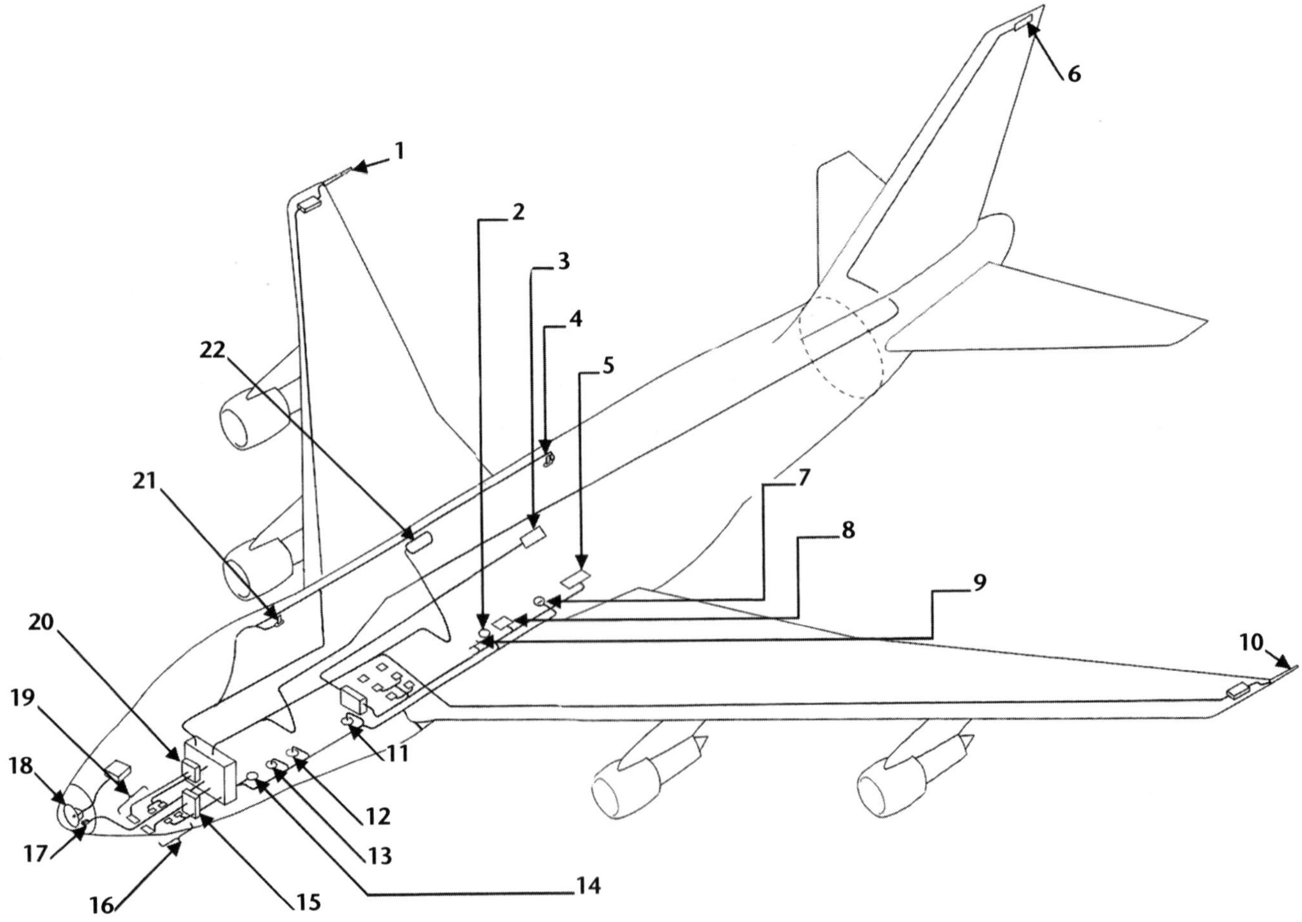

Chapter 2: Power Distribution Digital and Data Bus Systems

FILL IN THE BLANK QUESTIONS

name:

date:

1. An aircraft's power distribution system is comprised of one or more electrical distribution points. These distribution points are often made of a solid copper bar referred to as a ____________ or ____________.

2. On most transport category aircraft, units known as ____________ are used to convert AC to DC and supply direct current to the aircraft.

3. The four data word formats that conform to the ARINC 429 standard are: ____________, ____________, ____________, ____________.

4. There are three basic types of power distribution systems found on transport category aircraft, the ____________, ____________ and the ____________.

5. A ____________ power distribution system is used on modern four-engine aircraft such as the Boeing 747-400.

6. The ____________ is a device used on many twin-engine transport category aircraft to supply emergency hydraulic and electrical power.

7. The ____________ power distribution system is typically found on twin-engine transport category aircraft and maintains two isolated electrical distribution systems.

8. The ____________ is a three engine aircraft that employs a parallel power distribution system.

9. ____________ electrical power distribution system can operate with all generators in parallel or can isolate the left and right generators when needed.

10. On the B-747-400, the AC ground handling (GH) busses are powered by closing the ground handling relay (GHR) to either the ____________ or ____________ power sources.

11. On the B-747-400, the ground service (GS) busses are controlled from the ____________ station located at the number two left door of the aircraft.

12. To change the AC power source without interruption in electrical power the B-747-400 incorporates an automated system called the ____________.

13. The Boeing 777 contains a total of ____________ (insert number) engine driven generators and ____________ (insert number) generator driven by the ram air turbine.

14. B-777's two backup generators are variable ____________ constant ____________ units.

Chapter 2: Power Distribution Digital and Data Bus Systems

FILL IN THE BLANK QUESTIONS

name:

date:

15. The A-380 employs six engine-driven AC generators; the main engines drive four and the other two are driven by the ______________________.

16. The B-787 employs ______________ (insert number) main engine starter generators, and ______________ APU starter generators with a combined output of ______________ megawatts of electrical power.

17. The three A-380 maintenance access terminals are known as: the ______________________ (OMT), ______________________ (OIT), and ______________________ (PMAT).

18. The ______________________ (CCU) connects each section of the computer to coordinate control of all activities of that system. The CCU receives its instructions from the ______________________ (CPU).

19. Most digital data is transmitted one binary digit at a time. This is referred to as ______________ data transmission.

20. The device that converts parallel data into serial form is called a ______________ circuit. The circuit used to convert serial data into parallel form is called a ______________________.

21. The ______________ is a light filter made of extremely fine lines and used as a major control element in all LCDs.

22. The most common flat panel display found on aircraft is the ______________________.

23. An LCD with a high display resolution means there is an increased number of ______________ per square inch, compared to a low resolution display.

24. The LCD dynamic driver known as an ______________________ is typically used for aircraft instrument and other displays requiring a fast update rate.

25. ______________________ is the movement of electrons created when a material containing a static charge comes in contact with a material containing a different or neutral charge.

26. At the workstation, ESDS components should never be set directly on to the tabletop. The workstation should be equipped with either a conductive or ______________________ mat.

27. Hexadecimal values are base ______________ numbers.

28. An ______________ air blower will safely delete any static charge formed on nonconductors.

29. A component failure caused by static discharge that creates an immediate system defect is known as a ______________ failure.

Chapter 2:

Power Distribution Digital and Data Bus Systems

FILL IN THE BLANK QUESTIONS

name:

date:

30. A component that experienced a soft failure due to electrostatic discharge is often said to be ________________ .

31. Octal numbers are base eight and therefore comprised of eight different symbols; they are ________________ (insert number).

32. Hexadecimal notation is comprised of a series of ________________ (insert number) bit groups.

33. The hexadecimal numbering system is comprised of ____________ (insert number) symbols and they are: ________________ (insert numbers/letters).

34. ________________ is a global corporation owned by U.S. and international airlines and aircraft operators. The company provides services related to a variety of aviation communication and navigation systems.

35. The three most commonly used ARINC digital data bus standards are: ________________, ________________, and ________________ .

36. Two common data bus system found on corporate-type aircraft are the ________________ and ________________ .

37. The Manchester Code is a serial digital data transfer system that incorporates a ________________ change in each data bit.

38. A ________________ connector contains two or more parallel rows of pins or sockets surrounded by a D-shaped metal shell.

39. ASCB is a bi-directional data bus operating at ____________ MHz (insert number). This system uses multiple bus controllers, which coordinate bus transmission activities.

40. The ASCB request/answer time periods are known as ________________ .

41. The Commercial Standard Digital Bus (CSDB) is a one-way data bus system between one transmitter and a maximum of ____________ (insert number) receivers.

42. The CSDB data bus standard allows for data transmission in one of three forms: ________________, ________________, and ________________ .

43. The CSDB data bus system operates at a high speed of ________________ or a low speed of ________________ .

44. In the CSDB data bus format, the ________________ is a specific serial message, consisting of a defined number of bytes.

Chapter 2: Power Distribution Digital and Data Bus Systems

FILL IN THE BLANK QUESTIONS

name:

date:

45. Each ARINC 429 transmitter contains an internal clock; the timing signal is transmitted to each receiver via a null voltage in each data bit. The bus voltage reverses polarity to change from binary 1 to binary 0. This type of data transmission is referred to as ________________.

46. The ARINC 429 system provides for the transmission of ____________ (insert number) bits in each byte, or word.

47. The ARINC 629 data signal begins in Manchester format and is converted to a ________________ for transmission on the data bus.

48. The ARINC 429 standard assigns the first 8 bits of a 32-bit word as the ________________, and bit number 32 as a ________________.

49. The parity bit of the ARINC 429 code is included to permit error checks by the ARINC receiver. The receiver also performs a ________________, which deletes any unreasonable information that may be transmitted on the bus.

50. The ARINC 429 AIM word format is comprised of three types of data files, the ________________, ________________, and ________________.

51. The ARINC 429 ________________ word format is used to transmit the status of several individual components or systems.

52. Data bits not used to transmit information in the ARINC 429 data field are referred to as ________________ and are set to binary 0.

53. The ARINC 429 discrete word format uses bits ____________ (insert number) through ____________ for the data field and assigns bits 30 and 31 for the SSM.

54. ARINC ____________ (insert number) is a digital data bus format that permits up to 120 receiver/transmitters to share a bi-directional serial data bus that can be up to 100 meters long.

55. ARINC 629 operates at a speed of ____________ (insert number) megabits/second.

56. A doublet signal is a short positive or short negative pulse transmitted on the data bus whenever a data value changes from ________________ to ________________.

57. In the ARINC 629 data bus structure, the ________________ is the first interface between the transmitting (or receiving) LRU and the data bus.

58. The Serial Interface Module changes the Manchester current signal from the LRU into a ________________.

Chapter 2:
Power Distribution Digital and Data Bus Systems

FILL IN THE BLANK QUESTIONS

name:

date:

59. The stub cable is a four-wire cable used to connect the Terminal Controller to the Current Mode Coupler, and can be a maximum of ____________ (insert number) feet long.

60. The ______________________ is an inductive coupling device that connects the LRU to the 629 data bus.

61. On a 629 data bus, the ______________________ is a time period common to all users. This gap can be thought of as the reset signal for the transmitters.

62. The ____________________ is a common time period, between 0.5 and 64 milliseconds long for all ARINC 629 transmitters.

63. The ____________________ is a unique time period for each transmitter on the ARINC 629 data bus.

64. The I/O processor found in the AFDX data bus system is used to direct ______________ from the incoming (RX) buffers to the appropriate outgoing (TX) buffers.

65. The ____________________ is the digital identifier used to direct all packets within the network.

66. The ________________ of the AFDX system defines which port will be used to receive/transmit data.

67. AFDX sampling ports can only contain ____________ (insert number) data packet in the queue.

68. The ______________________ is a common test instrument used to receive and transmit digital data for the purpose of troubleshooting digital systems.

69. The data bus fault known as ________________ occurs when a portion, or portions, of the data signal are completely lost during transmission.

70. A data bus problem can affect the data signal in three common ways. The three common data bus faults are called: ____________, ____________, or ____________.

71. Data bus ________________ occurs when a digital data signal becomes weak or the transmitted voltage becomes too low.

72. Data bus ________________ occurs when an unwanted signal is induced into the system wiring and distorts the transmitted data.

73. There are two basic test instruments that can be used to detect the transmission and reception of digital data. These instruments are the ______________________ and the ______________________.

Chapter 2: Power Distribution Digital and Data Bus Systems

FILL IN THE BLANK QUESTIONS

name:

date:

74. A ______________________ allows the technician to display a given portion of a constantly changing digital signal for the purpose of system troubleshooting and analysis.

75. FIFO stands for ______________________.

76. A ______________________ occurs when the rise or fall time of the digital signal responds too slowly and the transmitted data is unusable.

77. ______________________ is a change of direction of a light beam.

78. ______________________ is the bending of light as it passes through two different materials.

79. Light traveling through glass fiber is called ______________________.

80. Optical fiber which carries the data signal is made up of three essential layers: the ______________________, the ______________________ and the ______________________.

81. ETFE is a polymer known as ethylene-tetrafluoroethylene made by DuPont under the trade name ______________________.

82. Attenuation is the signal loss from the transmitter to the receiver in ______________________.

Chapter 2: Power Distribution Digital and Data Bus Systems

MULTIPLE CHOICE QUESTIONS

name:

date:

1. The Beechcraft King Air uses direct current (DC) to power:
   a. The majority of the aircraft systems
   b. Only the DC ESS bus
   c. Only the main battery bus
   d. Both the right and left GEN buses; all other systems are AC

2. What type of power distribution system is employed on the Boeing 747-400?
   a. Split bus system
   b. Split-parallel system
   c. Parallel system
   d. Non-paralleling system

3. The Airbus A-320 uses what type of power distribution system?
   a. Split bus system
   b. Split-parallel system
   c. Parallel system
   d. Non-paralleling system

4. The Boeing 727 uses what type of power distribution system?
   a. Split bus system
   b. Split-parallel system
   c. Parallel system
   d. Non-paralleling system

5. The no-break power transfer system (NBPT) is found on what type of aircraft?
   a. A-320
   b. MD-11
   c. B-747-400
   d. B-727

6. What is the maximum output of the B-777 ram air turbine generator?
   a. 7.5 KVA
   b. 26 KVA
   c. 90 KVA
   d. 120 KVA

7. On the B-777 how often is the RAT generator operationally tested?
   a. Every 1,000 hours of aircraft flight time
   b. Every 6,000 hours of aircraft flight time
   c. Every 6 months
   d. Every 24 calendar months

8. What is the maximum output of the B-777 two main engine-driven AC generators?
   a. 90 KVA
   b. 115 KVA
   c. 120 KVA
   d. 150 KVA

9. What is the maximum output of the four main engine-driven AC generators used on the Airbus A-380?
   a. 90 KVA
   b. 115 KVA
   c. 120 KVA
   d. 150 KVA

10. Which of the following aircraft use generators that have a variable output frequency between 370 to 770 Hz?
    a. B-747-400
    b. A-320
    c. A-380
    d. B-777

Chapter 2:
Power Distribution Digital and Data Bus Systems

MULTIPLE CHOICE QUESTIONS

name:

date:

11. Which of the following aircraft use starter generators on the main engines?
    a. B-747-400
    b. A-320
    c. A-380
    d. B-787

12. On transport category aircraft, the external power applied to the aircraft for ground operation is typically ____________________.
    a. 28VDC
    b. 115V, 60Hz AC
    c. 115V, 60Hz AC
    d. 115V, 400Hz AC

13. In the power distribution system found on transport category aircraft, what unit is used to change 115V, 400Hz AC into 28VDC?
    a. Transformer rectifier (TR)
    b. Rectifier transformer (RC)
    c. Bus power control unit (BPCU)
    d. Generator control unit (GCU)

14. A major disadvantage of a reflective LCD is its ____________________.
    a. Large power usage
    b. Poor visibility in low light conditions
    c. Poor resolution
    d. Slow response time

15. What type of components are most likely to be damaged by electrostatic discharge?
    a. Bus power control units
    b. Data bus receivers
    c. CMOS devices
    d. ARINC devices

16. In order for a static discharge to be visible, it must be at least:
    a. 3,000 volts
    b. 5,000 volts
    c. 7,000 volts
    d. 10,000 volts

17. Which of the following should a technician wear when working on ESDS components?
    a. A grounding strap
    b. Rubber-soled shoes
    c. A direct connection to the electrical system ground
    d. Cotton and nylon clothing

18. How many binary bits are used in an Octal Notation group to create each octal digit?
    a. 2
    b. 3
    c. 4
    d. 8

19. How many binary bits are used in a Hexadecimal Notation group to create each hexadecimal digit?
    a. 2
    b. 3
    c. 4
    d. 8

20. Which of the following is a self-clocking, non-return-to-zero data format used on digital aircraft systems?
    a. ARINC 429
    b. Manchester
    c. ASCB
    d. CSDB

Chapter 2:

Power Distribution Digital and Data Bus Systems

MULTIPLE CHOICE QUESTIONS

name:

date:

21. Which of the following is a digital data bus system developed by Collins Avionics?
    a. ASCB
    b. Manchester
    c. CSDB
    d. ARINC

22. How many data bits are used to describe each character of the ISO-alphabet in the ARINC 429 AIM word format?
    a. 8
    b. 7
    c. 9
    d. 4

23. What is the maximum bus cable impedance and capacitance for Avionics Standard Communication Bus data transmissions?
    a. 125ohms -2ohms and 12 ± 2μf
    b. 125ohms ± 2ohms and 12 ± 2pf
    c. 125ohms -2μohms and 12 ± 2pf
    d. 125ohms +2ohms and 12pf

24. ARINC 429 uses what voltage level to represent binary 1?
    a. -5V
    b. +5V
    c. -10V
    d. +10V

25. Which of the following is *not* an ARINC 429 data word format?
    a. BCD
    b. Discrete
    c. RAM
    d. AIM

26. Which of the ARINC 429 data bus word formats is most likely to be used for transmission of information requiring large amounts of data transfer?
    a. Binary
    b. Binary coded decimal
    c. AIM
    d. Discrete

27. The ARINC 629 bus operates at what speed?
    a. 100 kilobits per second
    b. 200 kilobits per second
    c. 1 megabit per second
    d. 2 megabits per second

28. Which of the ARINC 429 data bus word formats is most likely to be used for transmission of information on the status of several individual components?
    a. Binary
    b. Binary coded decimal
    c. AIM
    d. Discrete

29. What is the maximum number of receiver transmitters that can be connected to an ARINC 629 data bus?
    a. 20
    b. 40
    c. 100
    d. 120

Chapter 2: Power Distribution Digital and Data Bus Systems

MULTIPLE CHOICE QUESTIONS

name:

date:

30. In regard to ARINC 629, the transmitter produces a (an) ________________ signal; that signal is then changed into a voltage doublet signal for use on the data bus.
    a. Analog
    b. Manchester
    c. CSDB
    d. Direct current

31. In regard to ARINC 629, a doublet signal signifies a change in ________________.
    a. Voltage
    b. Current
    c. Logic state
    d. Impedance

32. The ARINC 629 data bus uses the Current Mode Coupler as a (an) ________________ connection to the bus.
    a. Crimped
    b. Ring end
    c. Soldered
    d. Inductive

33. Which of the timing signals used by ARINC 629 acts as a "reset" for all transmitters?
    a. Terminal gap
    b. Synchronization gap
    c. Transmit interval
    d. Terminal interval

34. Which timing signal of the ARINC 629 data bus assigns priority to the transmitters?
    a. Terminal gap (TG)
    b. Synchronization gap (SG)
    c. Transmit interval (TI)
    d. Transmitter signal (TS)

35. According to the Periodic Aperiodic Multi-Transmitter bus format, any transmitter can only make one transmission per each ________________.
    a. Transmit interval
    b. Terminal gap
    c. Synchronization gap
    d. End gap

36. According to the Periodic Aperiodic Multi-Transmitter bus format, each transmitter must remain inactive until the ________________ for that specific transmitter is complete.
    a. Transmit interval
    b. Terminal gap
    c. Synchronization gap
    d. End gap

37. What is the default rate for the transmission of data on an AFDX bus?
    a. 10 Mbits/s
    b. 16 Mbits/s
    c. 100 Mbits/s
    d. 256 Mbits/s

38. What is the time delay called whenever data packets are stored in buffers waiting for transmission on an AFDX data bus?
    a. Port ID
    b. Data Storage Delay (DSD)
    c. Digital storage
    d. Jitter

39. How many data packets can be stored in the queue of a sampling port?
    a. One
    b. Two
    c. Three
    d. Four

Chapter 2:
Power Distribution Digital and Data Bus Systems

MULTIPLE CHOICE QUESTIONS

name:

date:

40. Full Duplex Ethernet interconnects are specified by which of the following specifications?
    a. ARINC 664
    b. RS-232
    c. RS-429
    d. ARINC 429

41. What is the minimum time interval between Ethernet frames transmitted on the same virtual link?
    a. 0 to 16 milliseconds
    b. 1 to 128 milliseconds
    c. 2 to 16 milliseconds
    d. 32 to 256 milliseconds

42. Which of the following occurs when a portion or portions of the data signal are completely lost during transmission?
    a. Interference
    b. A terminal gap
    c. Timing interval faults
    d. Drop outs

43. When viewing a data bus signal using an oscilloscope, what type of fault would be present if the digital waveform contained heavily rounded corners?
    a. Drop out
    b. Attenuation
    c. Capacitance
    d. Interference

44. What are the typical wavelengths employed in fiber optic transmissions?
    a. 400 and 1,250 micrometers
    b. 800 and 1,550 micrometers
    c. 440 and 1,250 nanometers
    d. 800 and 1,550 nanometers

Chapter 2: Power Distribution Digital and Data Bus Systems

ANALYSIS QUESTIONS

name:

date:

1. If the DC battery bus is shorted to ground and then isolated from the system, what power sources (not busses) can supply power to the DC essential bus: battery No. 1; only the emergency generator; only the external power source; battery No. 2, any generator and external power? Refer to Figure 2-2-7.

2. As shown in Figure 2-2-11, the AC ground service bus currently receives power from

   ____.

   Choose all that apply:

   External power 1

   APU 1

   AC bus number 1

   The AC ground service bus is not powered

3. Refer to Figure 2-2-11. In order for the AC ground service bus to receive power from the APU No. 1 ground service transfer relay would have to ________________________ (change position, stay in the same position?) and the ground service select relay would have to ________________________ (change position, stay in the same position?)

4. Reference Figure 2-2-15 of the textbook and list the five transformer rectifier units found on the A-380 aircraft.

5. According to Figure 2-2-16 of the textbook, how many starter generators are found on each engine of the Boeing 787.

Chapter 2:
Power Distribution Digital and Data Bus Systems

ANALYSIS QUESTIONS

name:

date:

6. Refer to Figures 2-2-25 and 2-10-3 to answer the following questions concerning the Attitude Heading Computer (AHC). The AHC is part of the Attitude Heading System (AHS). (Note: AHC No. 1 is found on the right side of Figure 2-2-25.)

a. What is the bit rate for the AHC No. 1 bus? ______

b. What plug number and pin numbers of the SDD connect to the AHC No. 1 data bus?

______

7. According to Figures 2-10-3 and 2-2-25, what is the pulse rise/fall time (and tolerance) of the signal coming from LB-GP bus 2? Bus LB-GP is found in the upper left portion of Figure 2-2-25.

8. Complete the following table by adding the values for the 3-bit octal groups.

DECIMAL VALUE	OCTAL VALUE	OCTAL NOTATION 3-BIT GROUPS
0	0	
1	1	
2	2	
3	3	
4	4	
5	5	
6	6	
7	7	
8	N/A	N/A
9	N/A	N/A

9. Convert the decimal number 68 to an octal number.

Chapter 2:

Power Distribution Digital and Data Bus Systems

ANALYSIS QUESTIONS

name:

date:

10. Convert the base ten number 206 into a BCD value.

11. Convert the decimal number 68 to an octal notation number.

12. Convert the octal number 54 to a decimal value.

13. Convert the binary number 10001100 to a hexadecimal value.

14. Convert the hexadecimal number 2E to a binary value.

15. According to Figure 2-9-10 of the textbook, the Ethernet Header of any received AFDX data packet is removed during which level of the protocol stack?

Chapter 2:
Power Distribution Digital and Data Bus Systems

ANALYSIS QUESTIONS

name:

date:

16. Explain why the ARINC 429 data in Figure 2-8-16 is considered to be free of any transmission errors.

17. If an ARINC 429 word had a label of 01101001, what is the label number in octal? (Note: The digit on the right of the given binary label is bit No. 1, bit No. 8 is on the left.)

ARINC 429 Data Word No. 1

Using the following ARINC 429 data word to answer questions 18-22.

Note the following apply:

1. BNR word format,
2. Range = 0 - 4096,
3. Significant bits = 15,
4. Resolution = 0.125,
5. Unit of measure = knots,
6. Parameter name = E-W velocity.

(bit No. 32) 11110000111000010100000010111111 (bit No. 1)

18. Record the following for the above data word (ARINC 429 data word No. 1). (Note: Record the appropriate raw data, 1s and 0s, for the parameters below.)

    a. Parity bit (P) ________________________

    b. Sign-status matrix bits (SSM) ________________

    c. Data bits ____________________________

    d. Source/destination identifier (SDI) ____________

    e. Label bits ____________________________

19. What is the decimal value (include units) of the data for the above data word (ARINC 429 data word No. 1)?

Chapter 2:

Power Distribution Digital and Data Bus Systems

ANALYSIS QUESTIONS

name:

date:

20. Which bit number(s) are pad bits in the above data word (ARINC 429 data word No. 1)?

21. Decode the label for the ARINC 429 data word No. 1.

22. For ARINC 429 data word No. 1, is the transmitted word valid or invalid?

ARINC 429 Data Word No. 2

Use the following ARINC 429 data word to answer questions 23-26.

Note the following apply:

1. BCD word format,
2. range = 0 -750,
3. significant digits = 4,
4. resolution = 0.1,
5. unit of measure = nautical miles,
6. parameter name = DME distance.

(bit No. 32) 01101000011001001000000001101101 (bit No. 1)

23. Record the following for the above data word (ARINC 429 data word No. 2). (Note: Record the appropriate raw data, 1s and 0s, for the parameters below.)

    a. Party bit (P) ______________________

    b. Sign-status matrix bits (SSM) ______________________

    c. Data bits ______________________

    d. Source/destination identifier (SDI) ______________________

    e. Label bits ______________________

name:

date:

24. What is the decimal value (include units) of the data for the above data word (ARINC 429 data word No. 2)?

25. Decode the label for the ARINC 429 data word No. 2

26. For ARINC 429 data word No. 2, is the transmitted word valid or invalid?

ARINC 429 Data Word No. 3

Use the following ARINC 429 data word to answer questions 27-30.

Note the following apply:

1. BCD word format,
2. range = 0 - 600,
3. significant digits = 5,
4. resolution = 0.01,
5. unit of measure = PSI,
6. parameter name = hydraulic pressure.

(bit No. 32) 100001011000000011100010010000001 (bit No. 1)

27. What is the decimal value of the data in the previous example (ARINC 429 data word No. 3)?

28. Decode the label for the ARINC 429 data word No. 3.

Chapter 2:
Power Distribution Digital and Data Bus Systems

ANALYSIS QUESTIONS

name:

date:

29. For ARINC 429 data word No. 3, is the transmitted word valid or invalid?

30. How many pad bits are used in the data field of previous data word (ARINC 429 data word No. 3)?

ARINC 429 Data Word No. 4

Use the following ARINC 429 data word to answer questions 31-34.

Note the following apply:

1. BNR word format,
2. Range = 0 - 2000,
3. Significant bits = 6,
4. Resolution = 0.1,
5. Unit of measure = LBS,
6. Parameter name = fuel quantity.

(bit No. 32) 00100110000000000000000011001010 (bit No. 1)

31. What is the decimal value of the data in the previous example (ARINC 429 data word No. 4)?

32. Decode the label for the ARINC 429 data word No. 4.

33. For ARINC 429 data word No. 4, is the transmitted word valid or invalid?

Chapter 2: Power Distribution Digital and Data Bus Systems

ANALYSIS QUESTIONS

name:

date:

34. How many pad bits are used in the data field (ARINC 429 data word No. 4)?

35. In Figure 2-8-29, if message A takes 10μs, message B takes 8μs, and message C takes 13μs, how much time will elapse between the end of the first message A until the start of the second message A?

36. Name the four layers of the fiber optic cable shown in the diagram below.

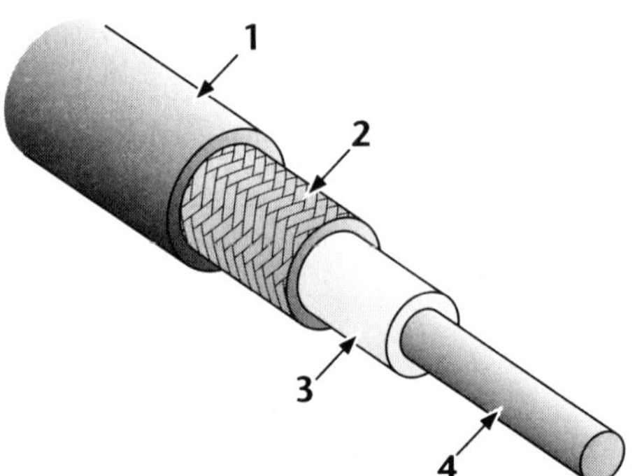

1. ____________________

2. ____________________

3. ____________________

4. ____________________

Chapter 3: Electronic Instrument Systems

FILL IN THE BLANK QUESTIONS

name:

date:

1. In order to reduce the number of wires required to operate EFIS, a ______________________ system is used to transfer a majority of information between the various components of the system.

2. The EFIS-85/86 is part of the Collins ______________________ series of avionics.

3. A five-tube EFIS-86 system consists of ____________ (insert numbers) electronic flight displays (EFDs), ____________ display processor units (DPUs), ____________ multifunction display (MFD), and ____________ multifunction processor unit, (MPU).

4. During the early '80s, the first transport category aircraft designed to employ EFIS was the Boeing ____________ and ____________ (insert numbers).

5. There are three types of control panels available for the EFIS-85/86, the CHP, DCP, and DSP. If only one control panel is used for the system it must be the ____________.

6. EFIS displays were used to replace conventional instruments, and various ______________________ annunciators.

7. The two CRT displays used by EFIS for flight and navigation information are called the electronic ______________________ and the electronic ______________________.

8. During normal operation of the EFIS-86, one Display Processor Unit (DPU) produces the necessary information to drive ________________ (insert number) CRT displays.

9. During ______________________ mode of the EFIS 86, one DPU can produce the necessary information to drive four EFDs.

10. There are eight separate circuit cards within the EFIS-85 DPU. The symbol generator card is divided into two separate functions, the ________________ generator and the ________________ generator.

11. There are three separate power supplies in the EFIS 86 DPU contained on ________________ (insert number) power supply circuit cards.

12. The acronym MFD stands for ______________________.

13. On the EFIS-85 the ______________________ is used to drive the MFD.

14. On five tube electronic flight instrument systems, the ______________________ is used to display weather radar data, course and flight plan information, and system checklist.

15. The MFD provides weather radar data, navigational maps, and ______________________ for checklists and maintenance functions.

Chapter 3: Electronic Instrument Systems

FILL IN THE BLANK QUESTIONS

name:

date:

16. The voltage required for normal operation of the EFIS-85/86 is between 29.5 VDC and 22.0 VDC. In emergency operations the EFIS will function with a voltage as low as ____________ VDC (insert number).

17. EFIS configuration ________________ is used to determine various display, input/output signal formats and other system parameters.

18. An electrical jack labeled DATA is located in the bottom right corner of the MFD. This jack is used to connect the ________________________ for page data entry.

19. A comparator ____________________ is displayed on one or more CRTs whenever two signals compared by the EFIS processors disagree.

20. A display on any EFIS CRT that is related to a complete or partial system failure is called fault ________________.

21. The EFIS-85/86 compact mode is often called the ________________ format.

22. The ________________ switches can be installed on the aircraft panel to bypass failures of the EFDs, DPUs, MPU, DCP, and/or the DSP.

23. The ________________________ is used to install new checklist data or modify an existing checklist stored in the MPU memory on the Collins EFIS-86.

24. Activity monitors are used to monitor each EFIS data bus to ensure there are a ____________________ at regular intervals.

25. If the EFIS EFDs detect an over temperature condition they will automatically ____________________ until the LRU cools to the appropriate temperature.

26. On the EFIS-86 the EHSI & EADI each receive power from the ____________ .

27. During troubleshooting of the EFIS-85/86 the ________________________ function is used to access real time data from the RAM memory of the DPUs and/or MPUs.

28. Each data field of the EFIS-85 bits mode is made up of 12 bits displayed in three groups of four. The least significant data bits are shown in the ________________ column.

29. The Bendix/King EFS-10 is a first generation system designed for ________________ and ________________ type aircraft.

30. The main processor unit for the EFS-10 is called a ____________________.

31. Radar data is transmitted to the EFS-10 symbol generator in the ARINC ____________ (insert number) format.

Chapter 3: Electronic Instrument Systems

FILL IN THE BLANK QUESTIONS

name:

date:

32. The five-tube EFS-10 system employs ________________ (insert number) symbol generators to drive the display units and provide system back up functions.

33. EFS-10 has a ________________ format that allows the technician to check system configuration, system strapping, radar straps, software codes, LRU status tests, and activate a test pattern.

34. The B-737 EFIS employs ____________ (insert number) symbol generators for system operation.

35. The B-737 EFIS symbol generators are located in the aircraft's ________________________.

36. The B-737-300 EFIS BITE information is accessed through the right or left ________________________, which is located in the center console between the pilot and copilot's seats.

37. On the Boeing 737, the symbol generator uses inputs from remote and local light sensors to adjust CRT ________________ .

38. An ________________ must be installed on any EFIS display in the EADI location and removed if the display is used as an EHSI.

39. The Collins Pro Line 4 avionics systems found on the Beechjet 400A aircraft uses an ________________________________ (IAPS), which provides integration functions for various avionics systems.

40. The PFD found on many integrated display systems combines the ____________ and ____________ displays on one CRT.

41. The ________________________ is used on the Beechjet 400A to display lateral navigation data, course map displays and radar information.

42. On the Pro Line 4 system, there are two back-up displays called Sensor Display Units (SDUs). The SDUs are monochrome displays used to show basic compass and ________________ data.

43. The ________________________ of the Beechjet 400A Integrated Avionics Processor System (IAPS) contains several line replaceable modules.

44. The ICC contains ____________ (insert number) environmental control cards that ensure a stable operating temperature for the line replaceable modules.

45. Initial fault isolation of the Beechjet 400A IDS is considered level ____________ (insert number) troubleshooting.

Chapter 3: Electronic Instrument Systems

FILL IN THE BLANK QUESTIONS

name:

date:

46. The ________________ page of the Pro line 4 IDS diagnostics is used to access a record of faults that occurred during previous flights.

47. The main processors for the B-747-400 IDS are called ________________.

48. The B-747-400 flight instrument displays are part of a complete aircraft monitoring system called the ________________.

49. All B-747-400 integrated display system BITE tests are accessed through the aircraft's ________________.

50. The flight displays found on the Airbus A-320 are part of an integrated display system called the ________________.

51. The ________________ is a system which allows pilots to view flight critical instruments while at the same time keeping their "head up" in order to view the area outside the airplane windshield.

52. There are two basic types of HUD systems; ________________ used by military and ________________ systems mounted between the pilot and the aircraft windshield.

53. First generation combiner-type HUDs use a ________________ to project an image on a phosphor screen.

54. Second generation combiner-type HUDs use a solid state light source, typically ________________ that are modulated by an ________________ screen to project an image.

55. Most of the HUD display is ________________, meaning that the information matches the outside world degree-for-degree.

56. ________________ was the first company to certify a synthetic vision system for a FAR part 25 certified aircraft.

57. The FAA approves ________________ (insert number) variations of electronic flight bag software; each provides different levels of sophistication, safety and reliability.

58. Electronic flight bags with ________________ software can only be used for static display applications such as a document viewer using a PDF or HTML format.

59. A typical Honeywell Primus display system uses ________________ (insert number) LCD displays for both flight and systems data.

60. The Primus 2000 IAC receives the majority of the input data from two ________________.

Chapter 3: Electronic Instrument Systems

FILL IN THE BLANK QUESTIONS

name:

date:

61. The Boeing 777's six flight deck displays receive their video information from the ______________________________.

62. The Boeing 777 PFDs receive inputs from four separate ______________ and receive video data on six ______________ cables.

63. The main backbone data bus for the Boeing 787 integrated avionics management system adheres to an ARINC ____________ (insert number) data bus standard.

64. The eight identical 15 by 20 centimeter liquid crystal displays found in the A-380 instrument panel are considered part of the ____________________ System.

65. The ______________________ is dedicated to present all warning information to the pilots in the event of a system malfunction.

66. Multiplexed video signals for the various displays on the A-380 aircraft are provided by the ____ unit.

Chapter 3: Electronic Instrument Systems

MULTIPLE CHOICE QUESTIONS

name:

date:

1. On the Collins EFIS 85, which of the following displays are capable of the rose, approach, and en route formats?
   a. PFD
   b. EHSI
   c. EADI
   d. MFD

2. On the Collins EFIS-85, which mode is active when one DPU is used to drive four EFDs?
   a. Isolated backup mode
   b. Reversionary mode
   c. Strapped mode
   d. Composite mode

3. Which of the following EFIS displays is used to show weather radar information and check list data?
   a. PFD
   b. EHSI
   c. EADI
   d. MFD

4. A five-tube EFIS-86 would have which of the following processors?
   a. Two MPUs and one DPU
   b. Two MPUs and two DPUs
   c. Three DPUs
   d. One MPU and two DPUs

5. At what temperature will the EFIS-85 EFDs automatically go blank to prevent damage to the system?
   a. 275 degrees Fahrenheit
   b. 320 degrees Fahrenheit
   c. 275 degrees Centigrade
   d. 320 degrees Centigrade

6. EFIS configuration strapping is used to determine which of the following?
   a. Various display formats and input/output signal parameters
   b. The number of EFIS display units used in the system
   c. The size of the EHSI display
   d. To program the MFD checklist data

7. Which of the following EFIS-86 displays employs a joystick used to aid in the entry of way-point data?
   a. PFD
   b. EHSI
   c. EADI
   d. MFD

8. On the EFIS-86, when does a comparator warning occur?
   a. Whenever two signals compared by the EFIS processors disagree.
   b. Whenever two displays have different formats.
   c. Whenever the DPU is comparing data with the MPU
   d. When the pilot's side DPU receives data from a copilot's side system.

9. When one EFD fails and the data is transferred to the operable EFD, the EFIS-86 is said to be in which of the following formats?
   a. Composite format
   b. Reversionary format
   c. Compact format
   d. BITS mode format

10. The Collins remote data programmer is used to:
    a. Upgrade the systems operational software
    b. Upgrade the systems airport database
    c. Download data from BITS mode
    d. Upgrade checklist data for the MFD

Chapter 3: Electronic Instrument Systems

MULTIPLE CHOICE QUESTIONS

name:

date:

11. The self-test function of the EFIS-86 is comprised of two modes. These modes are called:
    a. RAM monitor tests and BITS mode
    b. Confidence test and diagnostics/maintenance routines
    c. Checksum tests and BITS mode
    d. On-line monitoring and confidence tests

12. What software feature is used to monitor an EFIS data bus to ensure data transmission at regular intervals?
    a. Activity monitors
    b. BITS mode
    c. Checksum monitors
    d. Confidence tests

13. What is the lowest voltage for emergency system operations of the EFIS-86?
    a. 28 VDC
    b. 14 VDC
    c. 18 VDC
    d. 13.5 VDC

14. Which of the following statements best describes the EFIS-86 BITS mode?
    a. BITS mode is used to access fault history data from the RAM memory of the DPUs and/or MPUs.
    b. BITS mode is used to access real time data from the RAM memory of the DPUs and/or MPUs.
    c. BITS mode is used to access real time data from the RAM memory of the EFDs.
    d. BITS mode is used to access fault history data from the RAM memory of the EFDs.

15. On the Collins EFIS-86, how many bits of data are contained in each BITS mode data field?
    a. 1
    b. 4
    c. 12
    d. 32

16. What is the name of the processor units used on the Bendix/King EFS-10?
    a. Symbol generators
    b. Character generators
    c. Display processor units
    d. Multifunction processor units

17. The majority of information sent to the symbol generators of the B-737-300 EFIS is transmitted in which of the following formats?
    a. ARINC 629
    b. ARINC 453
    c. Analog format
    d. ARINC 429

18. During normal operation of the B-737-300 EFIS, symbol generator number one typically drives which display(s)?
    a. The right and left side EADIs
    b. The right and left side EHSIs
    c. The right side EHSI and EADI
    d. The left side EADI and EHSI

19. On the B-737-300 EFIS, if a color gun should fail on a CRT, that CRT will:
    a. Go blank
    b. Display a CRT failure fault flag
    c. Change to a monochromatic mode
    d. Divert all data to the other CRT

20. Generally speaking, second generation electronic instrument systems:
    a. Are more integrated than first generation systems
    b. Are found only on transport category aircraft
    c. Contain eight CRT displays
    d. Are designed for use on light aircraft

Chapter 3: Electronic Instrument Systems

MULTIPLE CHOICE QUESTIONS

name:

date:

21. The PFD found on second generation electronic instrument systems is a combination of which of the following instruments?
    a. HSI and ADI
    b. HSI and Compass
    c. ADI and Compass
    d. ADI and MFD

22. The Pro Line 4 Instrument Display System installed in the Beechjet 400A contains which of the following display configurations?
    a. One PFD, one ND, and two MFDs
    b. Two PFDs, one ND and one MFD
    c. One PFD, two NDs and one MFD
    d. Two PFDs and two NDs

23. On the Beechjet 400A IDS there are two backup monochrome displays used to show basic compass and navigational data in the event of a primary system failure. What are these displays called?
    a. Multifunction Display Units (MFD)
    b. Sensor Display Units (SDU)
    c. Supplemental Flight Displays (SFD)
    d. Integrated Supplemental Display (ISD)

24. Which of the following is true concerning the Integrated Avionics Processor System (IAPS) used on the Pro Line 4 IDS?
    a. IAPS is used on the latest version of the Collins EFIS-86.
    b. The IAPS is divided into four quadrants: 1A, 1B, 2A, and 2B. Each quadrant contains two power supplies.
    c. Two input/output (I/O) data concertrators are used to control all data entering leaving IAPS.
    d. IAPS contains six modules: FMC, CDC, FCC, ATC, IOC, PWR.

25. The PFDs on the Beechjet 400A each receive critical data directly from which of the following systems?
    a. The left and right flight management computers
    b. The attitude heading computers and air data computers
    c. The right side multifunction display processor
    d. The radio tuning units

26. How many categories of avionics troubleshooting are incorporated in the Beechjet 400 integrated display system?
    a. 1
    b. 2
    c. 3
    d. 4

27. Which troubleshooting page is used to display real time systems/subsystems failure data on the Proline 4 IDS?
    a. RU Diagnostic Data
    b. LRU Fault History
    c. System Status
    d. Avionics Status

28. How many electronic interface units are used to process data on the B-747-400 integrated display system?
    a. 1
    b. 2
    c. 3
    d. 4

Chapter 3: Electronic Instrument Systems

MULTIPLE CHOICE QUESTIONS

name:

date:

29. The display management computers found on the A-320 receive a majority of their data from which two LRUs?
    a. The Flight Warning Computer (FWC) and the System Data Acquisition Concentrators (SDAC)
    b. The Central Maintenance Computer (CMC) and the Electronic Interface Unit (EIU)
    c. The Display Electronic Unit (DEU) and the Flight Warning Computer (FWC)
    d. The Electronic Interface Unit (EIU) and the System Data Acquisition Concentrators (SDAC)

30. Which level of FAA approved software allows an electronic flight bag to employ dynamic interactive displays and processor units?
    a. Type A
    b. Type B
    c. Type C
    d. Type D

31. Where are the electronic flight bag (EFB) displays located on the Boeing 787?
    a. On the side console to the left of the pilot and to the right of the copilot.
    b. In the center console between the two pilots.
    c. The EFB data is displayed on the MFD on the main instrument panel.
    d. EFB data is displayed on a portable access terminal.

32. An FAA operational approval for electronic flight bags is required for all aircraft which operate under which FAR(s)?
    a. FAR part 21
    b. FAR part 65
    c. FAR part 65 & 135
    d. FAR part 135 & 121

33. How many LCD flat panel displays are used on the Garmin G1000 system found on Cirrus SR-22 aircraft?
    a. 1
    b. 2
    c. 3
    d. 4

34. What type of data bus is used for cross-talk between the PFD and the MFD on the Garmin G1000 system found on Cirrus SR-22 aircraft?
    a. ARINC 429
    b. RS-232
    c. A high-speed Ethernet bus
    d. ARINC 629

35. What device is used to input software updates on the Bendix/King KFD 840 system?
    a. An SD card
    b. A USB port
    c. A wireless connection
    d. A CD-ROM

36. Which LRU of the Primus 2000 is used to send data to the PFDs, MFDs and EICAS display?
    a. Attitude Heading Reference Unit (AHRU)
    b. Data Acquisition Unit (DAU)
    c. Control Display Unit (CDU)
    d. Integrated Avionics Computer (IAC)

37. Which system on the Boeing 787 integrates over 100 different LRUs into a central computing system employing Ethernet-based ARINC 664 (AFDX) technologies?
    a. The flight warning system
    b. The multiplexed video system
    c. The core processing input/output module
    d. The common core system

Chapter 3: Electronic Instrument Systems

MULTIPLE CHOICE QUESTIONS

name:

date:

38. Which ARINC specification is used to define the data interface to the electronic display units on the Boeing 787?
    a. ARINC 429
    b. ARINC 629
    c. ARINC 661
    d. ARINC 664

39. On the A-380 where are the alphanumeric keyboards used for CDS control located?
    a. On a fold-away table directly in front of each pilot
    b. Mounted to the yoke (control wheel) in front of each pilot
    c. In the center pedestal between the two pilots
    d. To the left of the pilot and the right of the copilot adjacent to the side stick controls

40. How many different modules are incorporated into the A-380 Core Processing Input Output Module (CPIOM)?
    a. 12
    b. 21
    c. 30
    d. 102

Chapter 3: Electronic Instrument Systems

ANALYSIS QUESTIONS

name:

date:

1. For the most part, all EFIS displays contain similar information. However, the specific layout of the display may change between systems. Label the following figures showing the various display features of a typical EADI and EHSI.

(A)

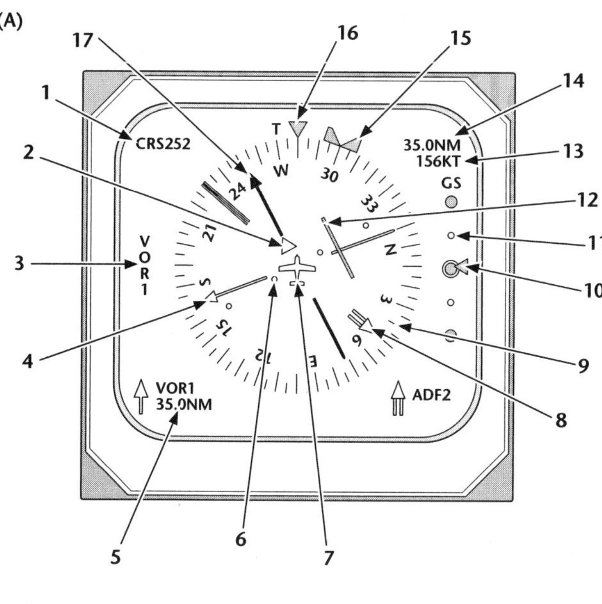

(B)

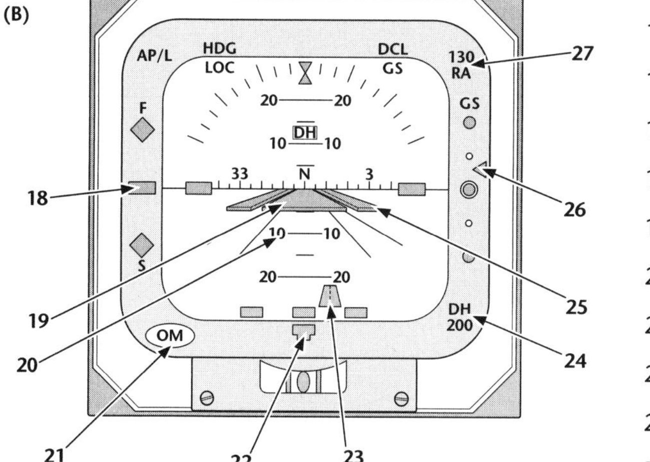

1. ______
2. ______
3. ______
4. ______
5. ______
6. ______
7. ______
8. ______
9. ______
10. ______
11. ______
12. ______
13. ______
14. ______
15. ______
16. ______
17. ______
18. ______
19. ______
20. ______
21. ______
22. ______
23. ______
24. ______
25. ______
26. ______
27. ______

2. According to textbook Figure 3-2-6, answer the following questions concerning the Collins EFIS-86. Include all voltage units.

   a. What is the screen voltage for the CRT display? ______

   b. What is the anode voltage for the CRT? ______

   c. What is the focus voltage for the CRT? ______

Chapter 3: Electronic Instrument Systems

ANALYSIS QUESTIONS

name:

date:

3. The Collins EFIS-85 and -86 employ various voltage values to operate certain sub elements of the system. Answer the following questions concerning the Collins EFIS-86 according to textbook Figure 3-2-7. Be sure to include all voltage units.

   a. List the voltage values sent to the EHSI and EADI from the A9 power supply card?

   ____

   b. What input voltage is sent to the A3 power supply card? ______________________________

   c. What voltage is output by the A3 card? ______________________________

4. Typically an EFIS process will receive a variety of input signals from various LRUs on the aircraft. According to textbook Table 3-2-1, what are the signal characteristics of the following DPU inputs?

   a. Marker beacon ______________________________

   b. Air data computer information ______________________________

   c. Pitch steering command ______________________________

   d. Vertical deviation ______________________________

Chapter 3:
Electronic Instrument Systems

ANALYSIS QUESTIONS

name:

date:

5. Name each LRU of the Collins five-tube EFIS shown in the following diagram.

   Choose from the following:

EADI	EHSI	MFD	WEATHER RADAR
DPU	MPU	CHP	DCP

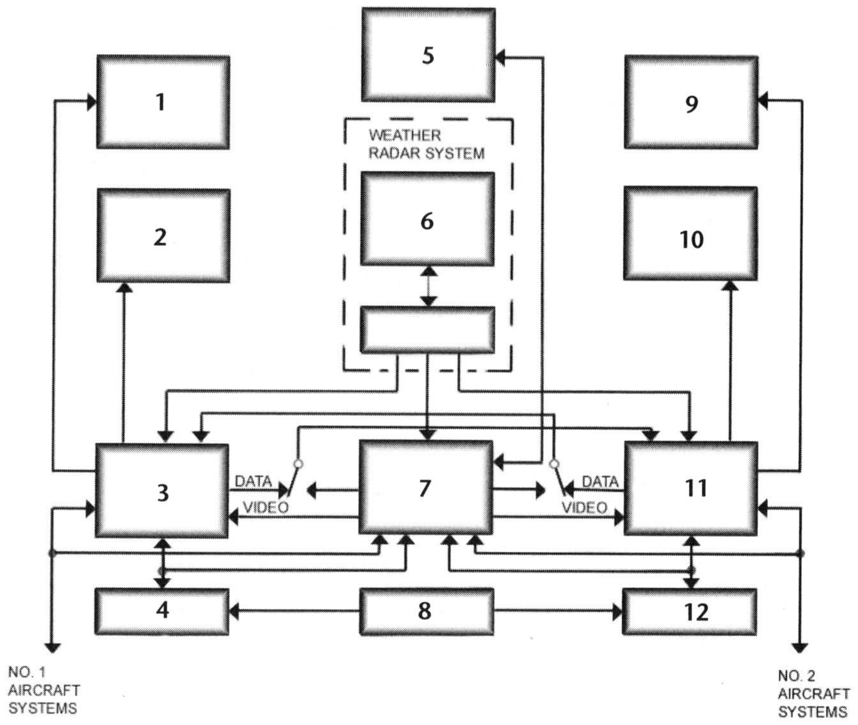

5
1
9
WEATHER RADAR SYSTEM
6
2
10
3
DATA
VIDEO
7
DATA
VIDEO
11
4
8
12
NO. 1 AIRCRAFT SYSTEMS
NO. 2 AIRCRAFT SYSTEMS

LRU IN DIAGRAM	COMPONENT ACRONYM/NAME
1	
2	
3	
4	
5	
6	
7	
8	
9	
10	
11	
12	

Chapter 3:
Electronic Instrument Systems

ANALYSIS QUESTIONS

name:

date:

6. Fault flags are used on most EFIS displays to indicate an inoperative system. List the title of the fault flags shown on the following EADI diagram.

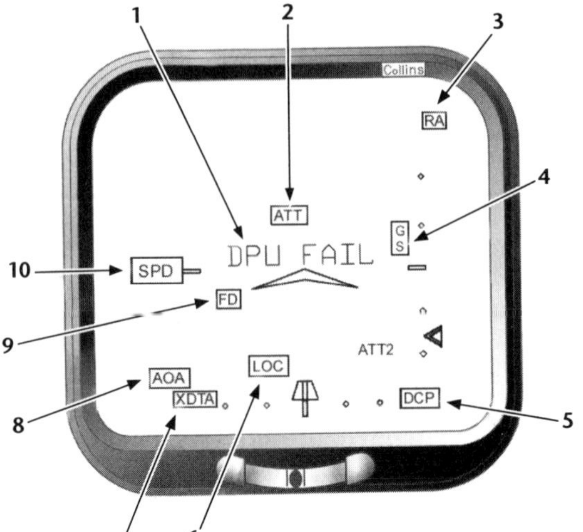

1. ______________________
2. ______________________
3. ______________________
4. ______________________
5. ______________________
6. ______________________
7. ______________________
8. ______________________
9. ______________________
10. ______________________

7. Collins EFIS-85 and -86 employ configuration strapping connections to "set" the EFIS processor to a given configuration. Strapping connections are set to binary 1 or binary 0. Referring to textbook Figure 3-2-29, assign a value to the following strap connections.

   a. If the autopilot installed on the aircraft is an APS-86 dual flight director, would the following pin connections be set to open or ground?

   DPU plug 2 pin 61 ____________ MPU plug 2 pin 1 ____________

   pin 115 ____________ pin 5 ____________

   pin 121 ____________ pin 9 ____________

   b. If the radio altimeter installed on the aircraft is an ALT-50, would the following pin connections be set to open or ground?

   DPU plug 2 pin 133 ____________ MPU plug 2 pin 61 ____________

   pin 134 ____________ pin 65 ____________

Chapter 3: Electronic Instrument Systems

ANALYSIS QUESTIONS

name:

date:

8. Aircraft manuals often contain flow charts to help the technician troubleshoot complex systems. The flow chart asks simple questions to guide the technician to the correct system repair. When following the troubleshooting flow chart of textbook Figure 3-2-30, what action should be taken if the following applies?

   a. One EFD is blank in DPU drive; both EFD illuminate in MPU drive. ________________

   b. All EFD illuminate, the MFD does not light, and the XDTA fault flag appears on the EFD. ________________

9. The BITS mode is used by the Collins EFIS-86 for in-depth troubleshooting procedures. Using Figures 3-2-34, 3-2-35, and Table 3-2-3 in the textbook, decode the following BITS mode messages.

   Decimal label No. 98 (true airspeed) bits are set to 0010 0011 1110:

   a. What is the value of the true airspeed data? ________________

   b. What are the units of the data? ________________

   Decimal label No. 98 (true airspeed) bits are set to 0000 1001 1000:

   c. What is the value of the true airspeed data? ________________

   Decimal label No. 97 (indicated airspeed) bits are set to 0111 0101 1000:

   d. What is the value of the indicated airspeed data? ________________

   e. What are the units of the data? ________________

10. Refer to textbook Figure 3-3-4 to answer the following questions concerning the display unit found on a second generation electronic instrument system.

    a. The video power supply receives input voltage from what component of the display unit? ________________

    b. What is the voltage (include units) of the video power supply screen and filament outputs? ________________

    c. What is the value (include units) of the anode voltage supplied to the CRT? ________________

    d. What component (or circuit) supplies the anode voltage to the CRT? ________________

Chapter 3:
Electronic Instrument Systems

ANALYSIS QUESTIONS

name:

date:

11. Integrated display systems found on late model aircraft interface with a variety of LRUs. On the following IDS diagram identify the components and record their names below.

Choose from the following:

Sensor Display Unit
Primary Flight Display
Integrated Avionics Processor Systems
Multifunction Display
Radio Tuning Unit
Control Display Unit
Navigational Display

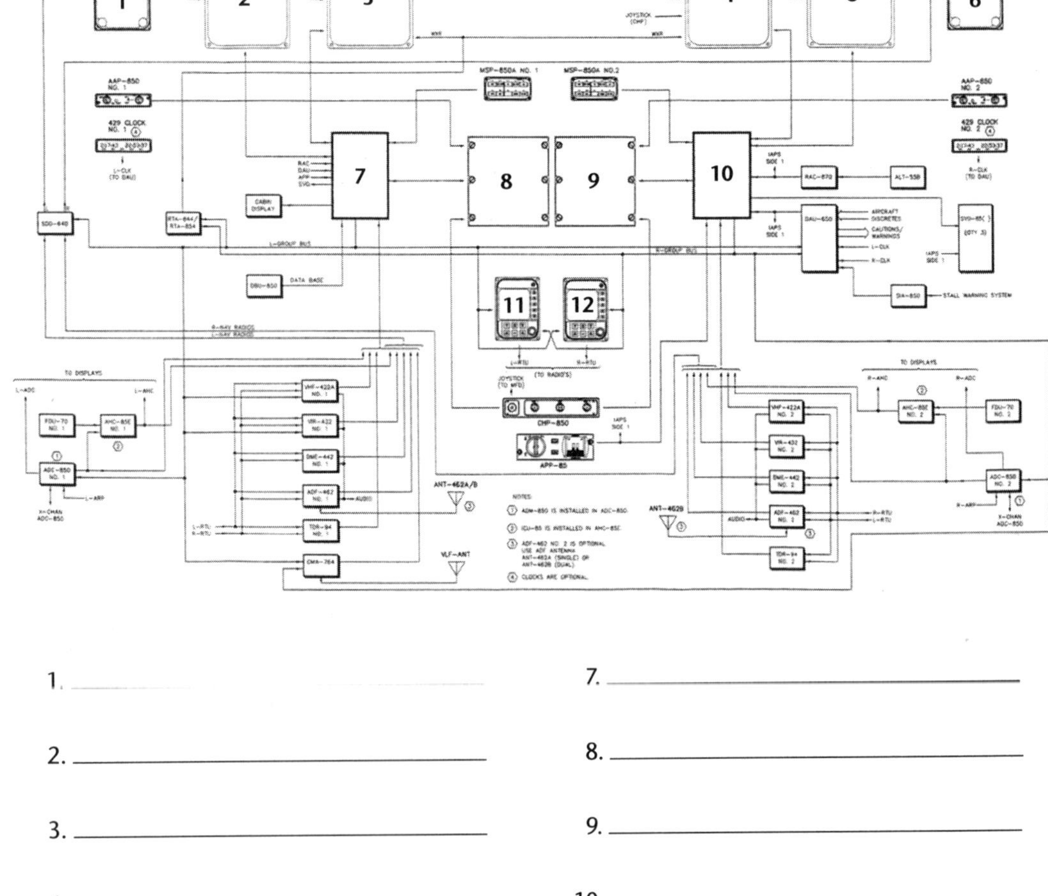

1. ______________________

2. ______________________

3. ______________________

4. ______________________

5. ______________________

6. ______________________

7. ______________________

8. ______________________

9. ______________________

10. ______________________

11. ______________________

12. ______________________

Chapter 3: Electronic Instrument Systems

ANALYSIS QUESTIONS

name:

date:

12. Refer to Figures 3-3-21 and 3-3-22 in the textbook to decode the following fault code. List all faults that apply to the given fault code. (Hint: Convert the hex number to binary values and evaluate the binary bits using Figure 3-3-21.

    Fault Code: (Hex format) 843200

13. Does the parity bit in the fault code for the previous question show correct data transmission, yes or no?

    Hints:

    - Assume the PFD DISPLAY diagnostic word is octal code 350. The Octal code 350 contains four bits set to binary 1 and is transmitted using bits 1 through 8 of the fault code data word.
    - The Octal code is not shown on the PFD during display of LRU Diagnostic Data.

Chapter 3: Electronic Instrument Systems

ANALYSIS QUESTIONS

name:

date:

14. On the lines below, write the components full name (not acronym) for the LRUs numbered in the following A-320 EIS diagram.

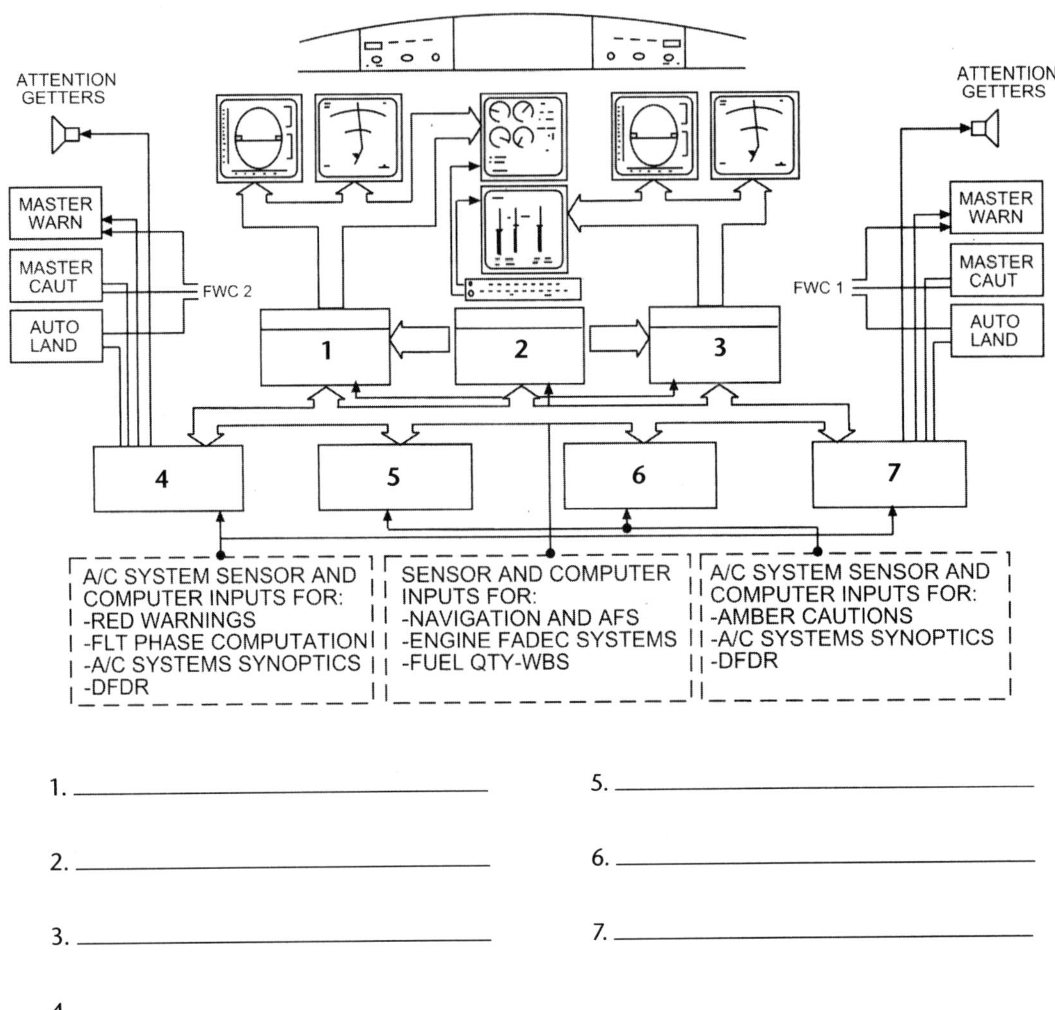

1. ____________________

2. ____________________

3. ____________________

4. ____________________

5. ____________________

6. ____________________

7. ____________________

15. According to Figure 3-4-12 in the textbook, which two units of the Garmin G-1000 system transmit data directly to IAU 1, IAU 2, the PFD, and the MFD.

Chapter 3: Electronic Instrument Systems

ANALYSIS QUESTIONS

name:

date:

16. Using the full name of the LRU, identify the five components numbered on the diagram below.

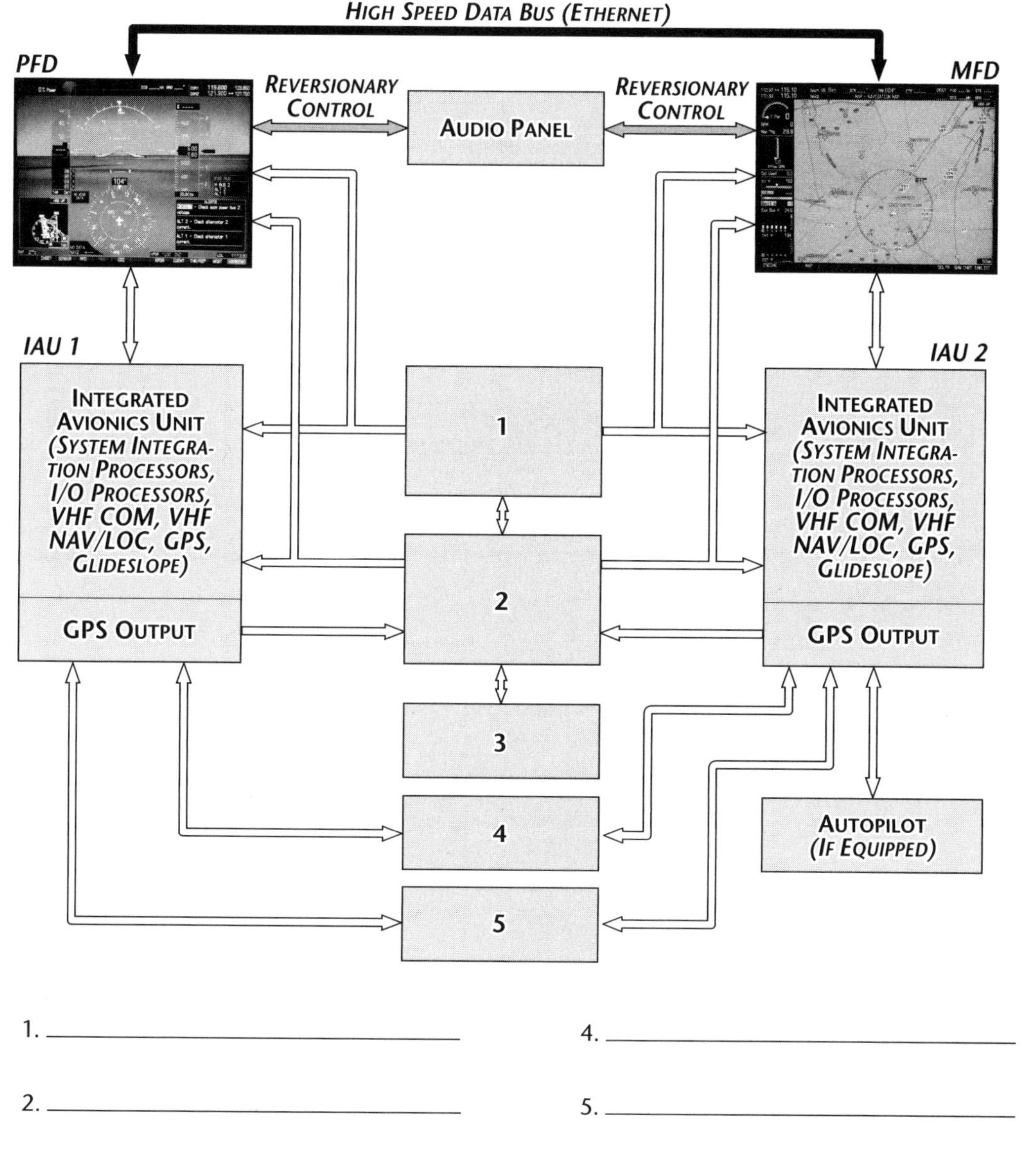

1. ______________________
2. ______________________
3. ______________________
4. ______________________
5. ______________________

17. According to Figure 3-4-18 of the textbook, what is the maximum number of GPS receivers supported by the KFD 840? ______________________

18. The Primus Electronic Display System (EDS) is made up of six major subsystems. How many of the following LRUs are included in the system? Record the number of LRUs found in a typical Primus 2000 system for each unit listed in the following table.

PRIMUN 2000 LRU	NUMBER OF LRUs IN THE SYSTEM
Integrated Avionics Computer (IAC)	
Electronic Display Unit (EDU)	
Guidance Panel Controller	
Data Acquisition Unit (DAU)	
Radio Management Unit (RMU)	
System Configuration Module	

19. According to Figure 3-4-21 in the textbook, what LRU transmits ARINC 429 data to the two radio management units?

20. According to Figure 3-4-31 in the textbook, what type of data bus system is used for data transmissions within the two Boeing 787 common core system cabinets?

Chapter 4:
Integrated Monitoring and Warning Systems

FILL IN THE BLANK QUESTIONS

name:

date:

1. The A-380 uses an indication and warning system known as ______________________________ ______________________________ .

2. The upper EICAS CRT is called the ______________________________ and the lower CRT is called the ______________________________ .

3. The EICAS Level A messages are known as ____________________; Level B messages are known as ____________________; Level C messages are ____________________; and Level D messages are called ____________________ .

4. The EICAS Level A messages are ____________________ in color; Level B messages are ____________________ .

5. The EICAS manual event mode is activated by pressing the ____________________ button.

6. The EICAS ____________________ mode will automatically record system parameters if a component or system failure occurs during flight.

7. To display systems data for maintenance purposes, EICAS employs a series of displays called ____________________ .

8. With only one EICAS CRT operable, the ____________________ mode will be used to display systems data.

9. On the B-757, two EICAS ____________________ are used to control the output data signals from the EICAS computers to the upper and lower CRT displays.

10. To verify malfunctions or analyze the systems monitored by EICAS a technician would access the EICAS ____________________ pages.

11. When using EICAS to verify which computer is receiving invalid or lost data, simply choose a specific computer using the display select panel. This technique is sometimes referred to as ____________________ .

12. The three main processing units found on the Boeing 747-400 integrated display system (IDS) are called ______________________________ .

13. The display units on the B-747-400 are called ______________________________ .

14. On the B-747-400 the ______________________________ will monitor the health of the various aircraft systems and record fault data for later access by maintenance personnel.

15. The ____________________ display is used to show one of the following formats: secondary engine data, status, synoptics, or maintenance pages.

Chapter 4: Integrated Monitoring and Warning Systems

FILL IN THE BLANK QUESTIONS

name:

date:

16. A concept known as ______________________ employs hard-wired, discrete inputs to establish specific aircraft/airline configurations for the B747-400 electronic interface units.

17. The B-747-400 EICAS allows for DSP control functions to be transferred to the ______________________.

18. The main and auxiliary EICAS displays can be transferred to either the pilot's or first officer's inboard IDU. Likewise the pilot's or first officer's PFD or ND can be transferred to the lower EICAS display. This transfer is controlled through the ______________________ modules and is typically done in the event of a display failure.

19. During normal operations, the B-747-400 EICAS utilizes two IDUs. These IDUs are known as the ______________________ and ______________________ displays.

20. The EICAS ______________________ format is used when both primary and secondary engine data is requested and only one display is operable.

21. On the B747-400, the ______________________ function of the CMC is used to determine the status of ARINC 429 data sent to the Electronic Interface Units (EIU).

22. The ______________________ system found on Boeing transport category aircraft is used to display aircraft system and engine parameters to the flight crew.

23. On the A-320, the two captain's side EFIS displays are called the ______________________ and the ______________________.

24. There are four basic types of information displayed by ECAM; ______________________, ______________________, ______________________, and ______________________.

25. On the A-320, the upper ECAM display is used for ______________________ and ______________________ (E/W) information; the lower display shows ______________________ and ______________________ pages.

26. The ECAM system incorporates two discrete visual annunciators located on the instrument panel glare shield. These annunciators are called the ______________________ and ______________________ annunciators.

27. The A-320 EIS contains three ______________________, which process data from the SDACs and FWCs.

28. Signals from the DMC to the display units are transmitted on a ______________________.

29. On the A-320, the two ______________________ computers monitor the various systems necessary to generate all warnings for ECAM.

Chapter 4:

Integrated Monitoring and Warning Systems

FILL IN THE BLANK QUESTIONS

name:

date:

30. On the A-320 ECAM system, the ______________________________ monitors aircraft systems, perform the necessary computations, and transmits output data to the FMCs and DMCs.

31. The installation of FWC No. 1 is distinguished from FWC No. 2 through a wiring practice known as ______________ .

32. The ECAM switching controls are used to select the ______________ of information to be presented on the EIS displays.

33. The ______________ section of the ECAM control panel contains 18 push-button switches used to access different systems for display on the lower ECAM CRT.

34. On an ECAM __________ page, it is easy to determine the real time status of a system.

35. The lower ECAM display will show one of three types of information: ______________, ______________ or ______________ during normal operation.

36. Five items are always displayed on the lower portion of the ECAM system/status page, this information is known as ______________ .

37. Each system failure displayed by ECAM can be identified as one of three major categories: ______________, ______________, or ______________ .

38. Corrective action messages are displayed directly below ______________ failure messages on ECAM.

39. For each system or component failure monitored by ECAM, a warning message is displayed on the E/W page. These warnings are divided into three ______________ and three levels.

40. ______________ warnings are always displayed on ECAM, and may also present a discrete aural and visual annunciator.

41. ______________ (ECAM) warnings always create an aural warning, and illuminate the red flashing master warning annunciators.

42. ______________ ECAM warnings are generated by failures that require immediate attention and possible future action.

43. ______________ messages have no related aural or discrete annunciator and occur mainly on component failures that are used for redundancy or emergency back-ups.

44. __________ messages appear on the status page of ECAM, but cause no flight deck effect.

45. __________ failure messages are recorded only by the aircraft's central maintenance system.

Chapter 4:
Integrated Monitoring and Warning Systems

FILL IN THE BLANK QUESTIONS

name:

date:

46. A ______________________ is considered any fault message presented on the specific control panel for a given system.

47. Items displayed by ECAM that are not system failures but still require crew awareness are called ______________________ messages.

48. On the A-320, the various segments of a typical flight are broken down into ten segments known as ______________________.

49. The Boeing 777 replaced the legacy ARINC 429 data transfer system with the newer ______________________ data bus.

50. The ECAM is part of the A-380 Control Display System (CDS) which contains two dedicated ECAM LCDs known as the ______________________, and the ______________________.

51. The Garmin G1000 shows all warning messages on the ______________________.

52. During normal operation on the Garmin G1000 system, the ______________ contains engine and airframe data on the left quadrant of the display.

53. If the Garmin display system experiences software errors related to an equipment configuration error a red ________ will be placed over the faulty system (or group of systems) on the PFD or MFD.

54. The system designed to reduce the incidence of mid-air collisions between aircraft is known as ______________________.

55. The two basic levels of TCAS equipment currently in operation in the United States are known as ______________ and ______________.

56. In a TCAS equipped aircraft a ______________________ is the first level of alert and given to the pilot if a potential midair collision is possible due to nearby aircraft.

57. Sirius XM WX weather satellites transmit information from the ______________________ ______________ through the satellite radio frequencies to aircraft Sirius XM receiver/ processors.

58. The system designed to help aircraft avoid controlled flight into terrain is known as the ______________________.

59. The modern standard for terrain avoidance systems is known as ______________________ ______________________.

Chapter 4: Integrated Monitoring and Warning Systems

MULTIPLE CHOICE QUESTIONS

name:

date:

1. The automated engine and systems monitoring process used on modern Boeing aircraft is called?
   a. EIS
   b. EICAS
   c. ECAM
   d. EFIS

2. What are the most critical EICAS alert messages?
   a. Warnings
   b. Advisories
   c. Alerts
   d. Cautions

3. Where are the EICAS master warning and caution annunciators located?
   a. On the main EICAS display
   b. On the PDF
   c. On the center pedestal between the pilots
   d. On the instrument glare shield directly in front of each pilot

4. What are the two major control panels used for the engine indicating and crew alerting system on the B-757?
   a. The EICAS control panel and the display select panel
   b. The display select panel and the maintenance control panel
   c. The maintenance control panel and the EICAS control panel
   d. The engine/status control panel and the maintenance control panel

5. What are the three basic display formats for normal operation of the early version engine indicating and crew alerting systems?
   a. Normal, secondary, and status
   b. Normal, auxiliary, and status
   c. Graphic, digital, and status
   d. Digital, status, and auxiliary

6. What information will always be displayed on the Main EICAS display?
   a. Compass rose and weather radar information
   b. Primary engine data
   c. Status, synoptics, or maintenance pages
   d. Secondary engine data

7. On the B-757, if both EICAS displays are inoperable, what is used to display primary engine parameters?
   a. The standby engine indicator
   b. Traditional electromechanical instruments
   c. A back up CRT display
   d. The data is transferred to a navigational display

8. What is the highest priority data to be displayed by EICAS? (i.e. What data will continue to be displayed in the event of a partial system failure?)
   a. Primary engine data
   b. Primary airframe data
   c. Engine fault data
   d. Engine and airframe system alerts

9. What are the two types of data stored in the EICAS nonvolatile memory?
   a. Verification and validation events
   b. Parameter and exceedance events
   c. Manual and automatic events
   d. Recording and capacity events

10. The B-747-400 EICAS is part of a complete aircraft monitoring system called the ________ .
    a. Electronic Interface System
    b. Intelligent Display System
    c. Central Maintenance Computer System
    d. Integrated Display System

Chapter 4: Integrated Monitoring and Warning Systems

MULTIPLE CHOICE QUESTIONS

name:

date:

11. The primary flight displays (PFD) are used to display flight data, such as the ________.
    a. Course map and compass rose
    b. Primary engine data
    c. Airspeed, pitch attitude, and altitude
    d. Secondary engine data, status, synoptics, or maintenance pages

12. The B-747-400 Electronic Interface Units (EIU) can accept up to 108 ARINC 429 data bus inputs. How many ARINC 429 data busses can operate at high speed?
    a. 0
    b. 108
    c. 56
    d. 8

13. Where are the primary flight displays (PFDs) located on B-747-400?
    a. The PFDs are located in the center of the instrument panel.
    b. Both PFDs are located on the pilot's side of the instrument panel.
    c. The PFDs are the outboard displays, one on the right, one on the left side of the instrument panel.
    d. The PFDs are the inboard displays, one on the right, one on the left side of the instrument panel.

14. The majority of digital data transmitted to the B-757 EICAS is transmitted in which of the following formats?
    a. ARNIC 429 data
    b. RS 232 data
    c. ARNIC 629 data
    d. ARINC 435 data

15. How many electrical pin connections are dedicated Pin programming on the B-747-400 Electronic Interface Units (EIUs)?
    a. 16
    b. 4
    c. 64
    d. 57

16. On the B-747-400, which alert and/or memo messages can be cleared from the EICAS display using the display select panel?
    a. Level A
    b. Level A, B , C , and D
    c. Level C and D
    d. Level B, and C

17. Which of the following systems is not displayed by the B-747-400 EICAS synoptic page?
    a. Flaps
    b. Gear
    c. Hydraulics
    d. Electrical

18. On the Boeing 747-400, what types of EICAS status messages will display real time data?
    a. Non-latched messages
    b. Latched messages
    c. Only ground maintenance messages
    d. Only in-flight maintenance messages

19. On the B-747-400, if one EICAS display is inoperable, what display format is used to show both primary and secondary engine data?
    a. Reversionary format
    b. Status format
    c. Compact-full format
    d. Synoptic format

Chapter 4: Integrated Monitoring and Warning Systems

MULTIPLE CHOICE QUESTIONS

name:

date:

20. The software data loader (SDL) used to update software in the B-747-400 IDS can be a carry on unit or permanently installed in the aircraft. If a permanent SDL is used, where is it located?
    a. In the forward electrical equipment bay
    b. In the center counsel of the flight deck
    c. In the overhead panel of the flight deck
    d. In the observers console on the flight deck

21. Where is BITE data displayed for troubleshooting the B-747-400 integrated display system?
    a. On the CDU
    b. On the main EICAS display
    c. On the auxiliary EICAS display
    d. On the PFD

22. What is used on the Boeing 757 to perform testing of the EICAS computers, upper and lower display units, the master caution and warning displays, and various EICAS interfaces?
    a. The EICAS MCP test
    b. The EICAS BITE test
    c. The pin programming test
    d. The EICAS DSP test

23. The electronic instrument system found on the A-320 employs how many CRT displays?
    a. 2
    b. 4
    c. 5
    d. 6

24. What system is used on the A-320 aircraft to monitor and display aircraft system and engine parameters?
    a. ECAS
    b. ECAM
    c. AIMS
    d. IDS

25. On the B-757 what signal format is used to transmit weather radar information to the EICAS displays?
    a. ARINC 453
    b. ARINC 429
    c. Analog video signals
    d. ARINC 629

26. On the A-320 EIS, which unit controls the master warning annunciators?
    a. SDACs
    b. FWCs
    c. DMCs
    d. CMCs

27. Which of the following are the two basic operational configurations of the A-320 ECAM?
    a. Manual mode and automatic mode
    b. Display mode and static mode
    c. Normal mode and mono mode
    d. Display mode and compact mode

28. What is the name of the top ECAM display on the A-320 EIS?
    a. The Primary Engine page
    b. The Engine /Status page
    c. The E/W display unit
    d. The Primary Status page

Chapter 4: Integrated Monitoring and Warning Systems

MULTIPLE CHOICE QUESTIONS

name:

date:

29. Sensors on the Garmin G1000 system collect engine and airframe data and send that information to which of the following?
    a. Directly to the MFD
    b. Directly to the PFD
    c. To specific warning annunciators and the PFD
    d. To one or both GEAs (Garmin Engine Airframe units)

30. During normal operation, where will the Garmin G1000 system display engine and airframe data?
    a. On bottom of the PFD
    b. On the engine display unit
    c. On the left quadrant of the display
    d. On the EICAS display

31. What is the highest TCAS alert level?
    a. Traffic advisory
    b. Alert advisory
    c. Collision advisory
    d. Resolution advisory

32. In modern aircraft, the TCAS display may be integrated with the
    a. Navigation display (ND)
    b. Multifunction display (MFD)
    c. Electronic horizontal situation indicator (EHSI)
    d. All of the above

33. The traffic collision avoidance system (TCAS) is required for all civilian aircraft that carry ________ passengers?
    a. 19 or more
    b. 30 or more
    c. 100 or more
    d. 4 or more

34. What visual display will be presented to the pilot in a TCAS traffic advisory alert?
    a. TRAFFIC displayed in yellow
    b. ALERT displayed in yellow
    c. TRAFFIC displayed in red
    d. ALERT displayed in red

35. EPGWS is required by the FAA for all turbine powered aircraft that carry ________ passengers?
    a. 4 or more
    b. 6 or more
    c. 12 or more
    d. 20 or more

Chapter 4: Integrated Monitoring and Warning Systems

ANALYSIS QUESTIONS

name:

date:

1. The first generation EICAS was found on the Boeing 757 and 767 aircraft. Insert the correct LRU name on the appropriate blank below for the components shown in the following Boeing 757 EICAS diagram.

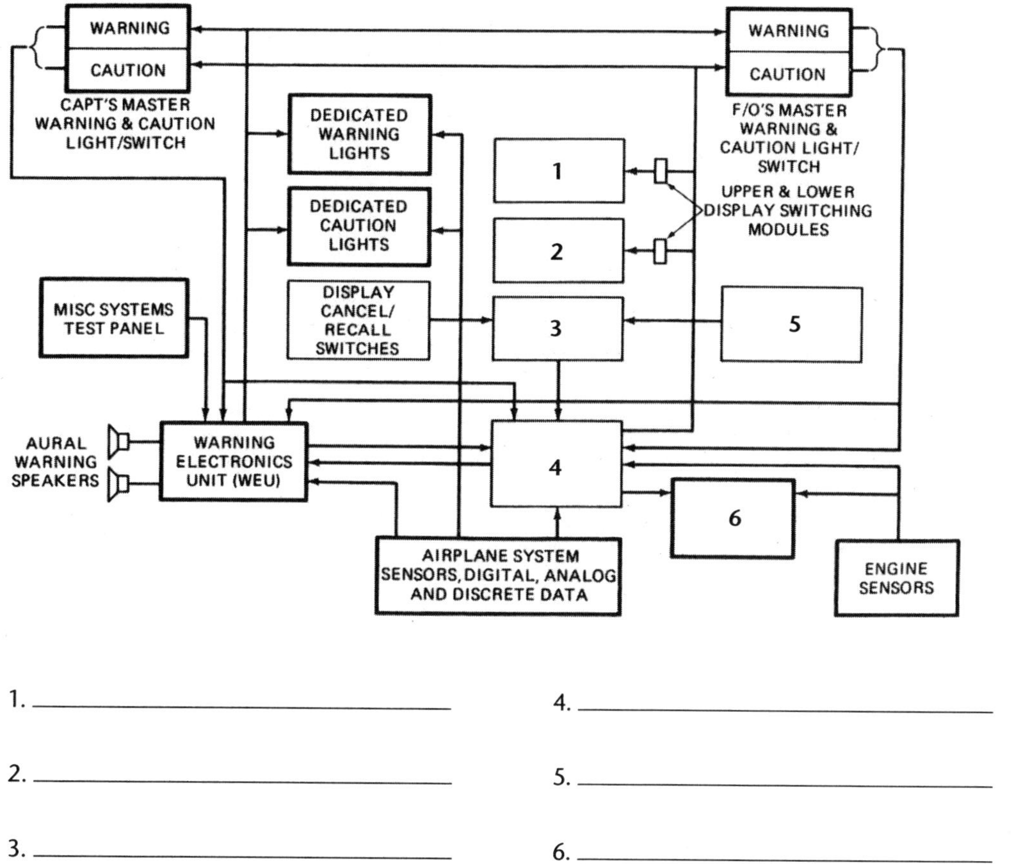

1. ______________________ 4. ______________________

2. ______________________ 5. ______________________

3. ______________________ 6. ______________________

2. Answer the following questions according to the EICAS block diagram in textbook Figure 4-3-4.

   a. Which EICAS computer sends data to the Captain's Master/Warning Light/Switch: the left EICAS computer, the right EICAS Computer, or both EICAS computers?

   ____

   b. The right hydraulic system sensors send information signals to which of the following: the left EICAS computer, the right EICAS computer, or both EICAS computers?

   ____

   c. What voltage is sent directly to the upper EICAS display? Include value and units.

   ____

   d. Define the location of the circuit breaker that sends power to the upper EICAS display? Include panel name and number. ______________________

   e. Are the Master Warning/Caution Light/Switch assemblies shown in their home diagram? (Note: Home diagrams are described in textbook Chapter 1.)

   ____

Chapter 4:

Integrated Monitoring and Warning Systems

ANALYSIS QUESTIONS

name:

date:

3. On the Boeing 757, the pilots use a Maintenance Control Panel (MCP) to input system commands to the aircraft EICAS. The following diagram shows a typical MCP. Use the provided table to insert the function of each switch shown in the following diagram.

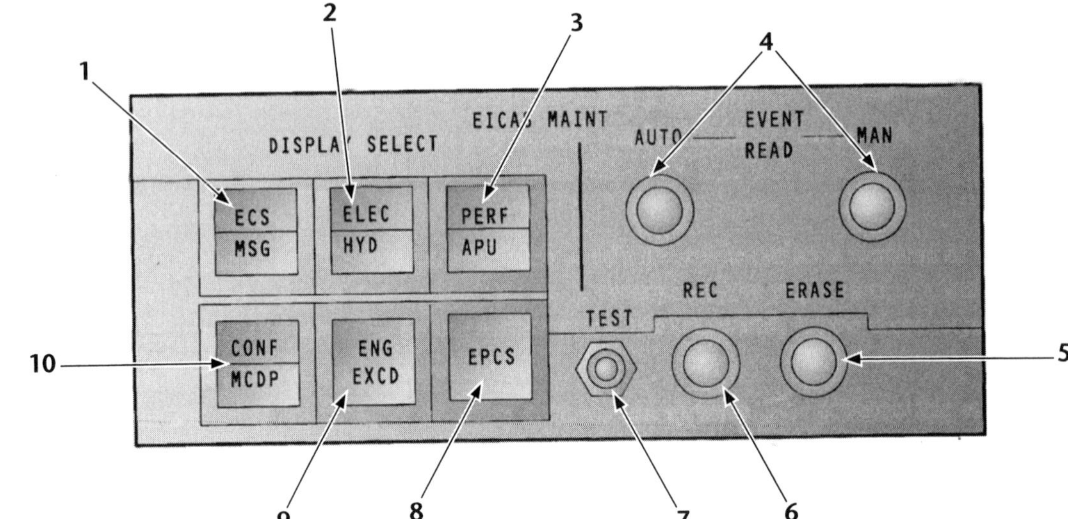

SWITCH NUMBER	SWITCH FUNCTION
1	
2	
3	
4	
5	
6	
7	
8	
9	
10	

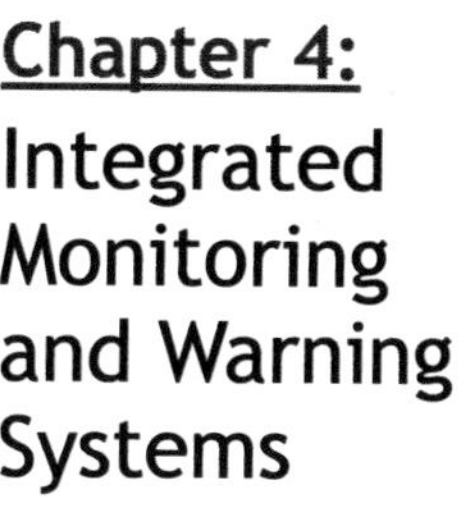

ANALYSIS QUESTIONS

name:

date:

4. For each numbered component in the following Boeing 747 IDS diagram, identify the display by name.

Choose from the following:

EHSI	PFD	MFD	EADL
Main EICAS	Main ECAM	Auxiliary ECAM	

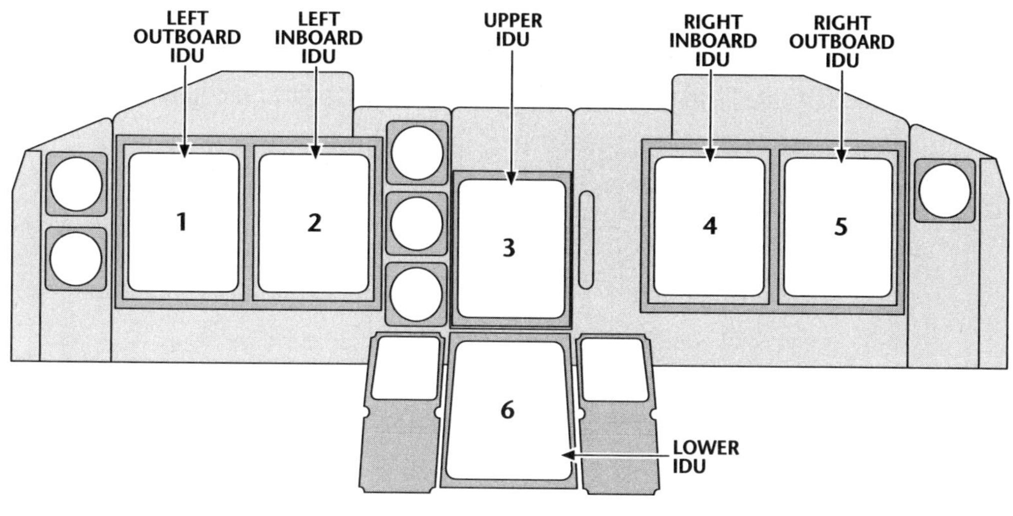

1. ______________________

2. ______________________

3. ______________________

4. ______________________

5. ______________________

6. ______________________

Chapter 4:

Integrated Monitoring and Warning Systems

ANALYSIS QUESTIONS

name:

date:

5. Answer the following questions according to the B-747-400 IDS block diagram in textbook Figure 4-4-5.

   a. How is the CDU weather radar data sent to the integrated display units: through the three EIUs; on a digital bus directly to three IDUs; through an analog connection to three IDUs; or through the EICAS display select panel?

   ____

   b. The right CDU sends digital data to which LRUs: all three EIUs, the right EIU only, the left EIU only, or the right and left EIU?

   ____

   c. The left CDU sends digital data to which LRUs: all three EIUs, the right EIU only, the left EIU only, or the right and left EIU?

   ____

   d. The right outboard IDU sends digital data to which LRUs: all three EIUs, the right EIU only, the left EIU only, or the right and left EIU?

   ____

Chapter 4: Integrated Monitoring and Warning Systems

ANALYSIS QUESTIONS

name:

date:

6. The B-747-400 Main EICAS display contains vertical gauges and digital data of various engine and airframe systems. In the table below, insert the type of data displayed on the main EICAS display shown in the following diagram.

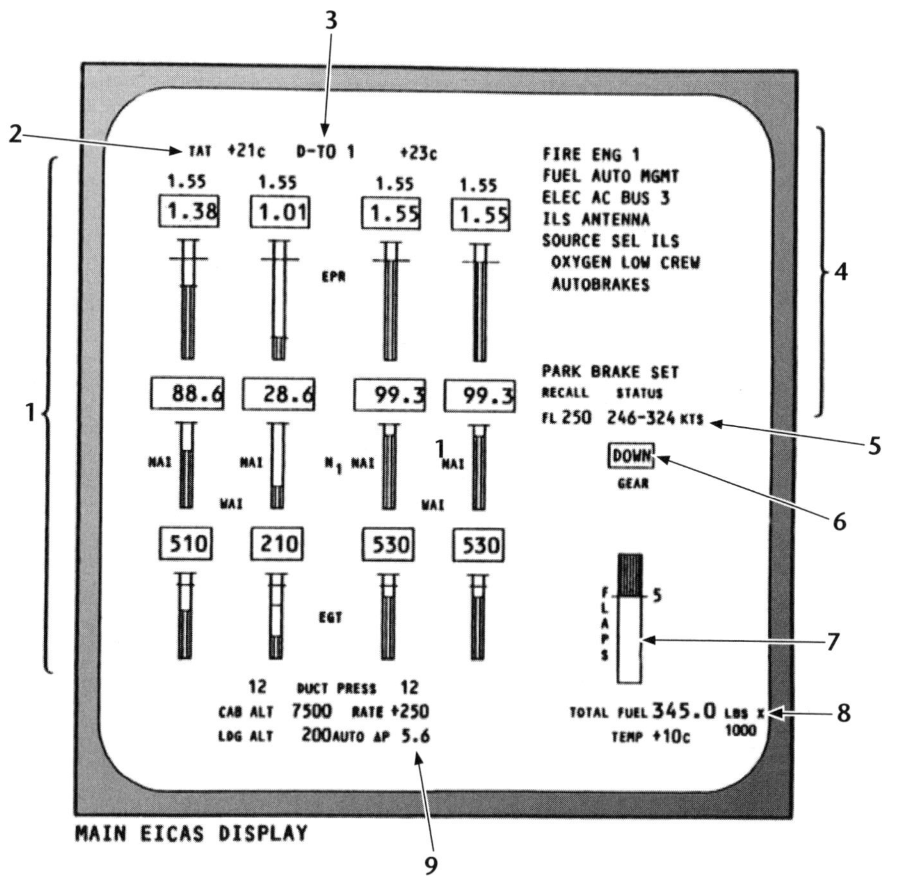

DATA NUMBER	TYPE OF DATA DISPLAYED
1	
2	
3	
4	
5	
6	
7	
8	
9	

Chapter 4:

Integrated Monitoring and Warning Systems

ANALYSIS QUESTIONS

name:

date:

7. Answer the following questions according to the IDS block diagram in textbook Figure 4-4-10.

a. Which bus feeds electrical power to the Upper IDU?

Bus name ________________________________

Voltage value and units ________________________________

Circuit breaker label ________________________________

The panel name/number where the circuit breaker is located ________________

____

b. Which bus feeds electrical power to the Right EFIS control panel?

Bus name ________________________________

Voltage value and units ________________________________

Circuit breaker label ________________________________

The panel name/number where the circuit breaker is located ________________

____

c. Which bus feeds electrical power to the left inboard IDU?

Bus name ________________________________

Voltage value and units ________________________________

Circuit breaker label ________________________________

The panel name/number where the circuit breaker is located ________________

____

Chapter 4:

Integrated Monitoring and Warning Systems

ANALYSIS QUESTIONS

name:

date:

8. The instrument panel of the B-747-400 contains a variety of displays and control panels related to the aircraft's integrated display system. These different panels and displays are typically referred to as LRUs. Insert the LRU name in the table according to the following Boeing 747 instrument panel diagram. Include the panel number, if applicable.

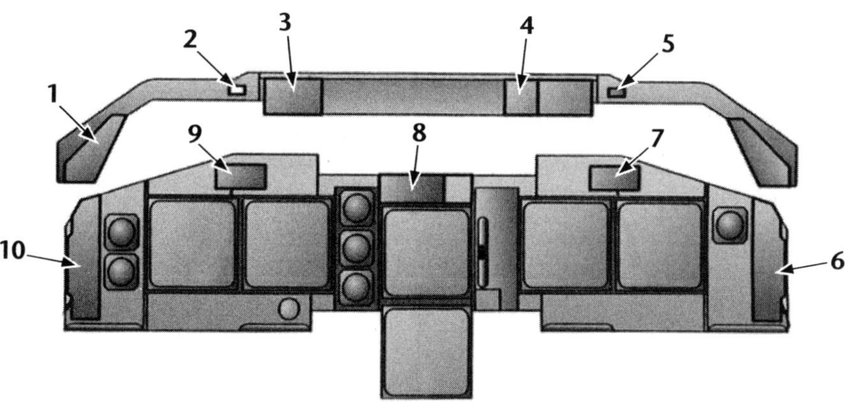

NUMBER	LRU NAME AND PANEL NUMBER (IF APPLICABLE)
1	
2	
3	
4	
5	
6	
7	
8	
9	
10	

Chapter 4:

Integrated Monitoring and Warning Systems

ANALYSIS QUESTIONS

name:

date:

9. There are 10 LRUs related to the operation of the A-320 electronic instrument system shown in the following diagram. Identify each LRU numbered on the diagram and write its name below on the corresponding blank.

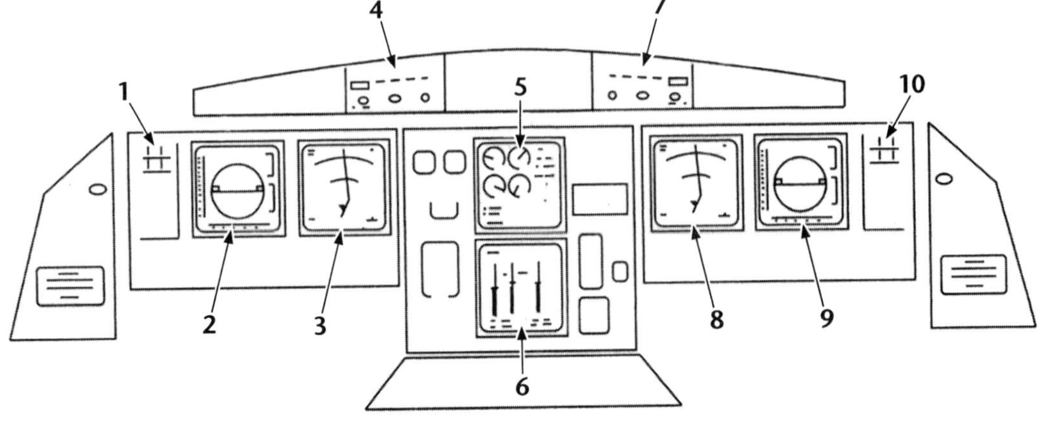

1. ______________________
2. ______________________
3. ______________________
4. ______________________
5. ______________________
6. ______________________
7. ______________________
8. ______________________
9. ______________________
10. ______________________

Chapter 4: Integrated Monitoring and Warning Systems

ANALYSIS QUESTIONS

name:

date:

10. There are six display units and seven computers found in the A-320 Electronic Instrument System. Write the correct LRU name below for the components shown in the following A-320 EIS interface diagram. Use the complete LRU name, not the acronym.

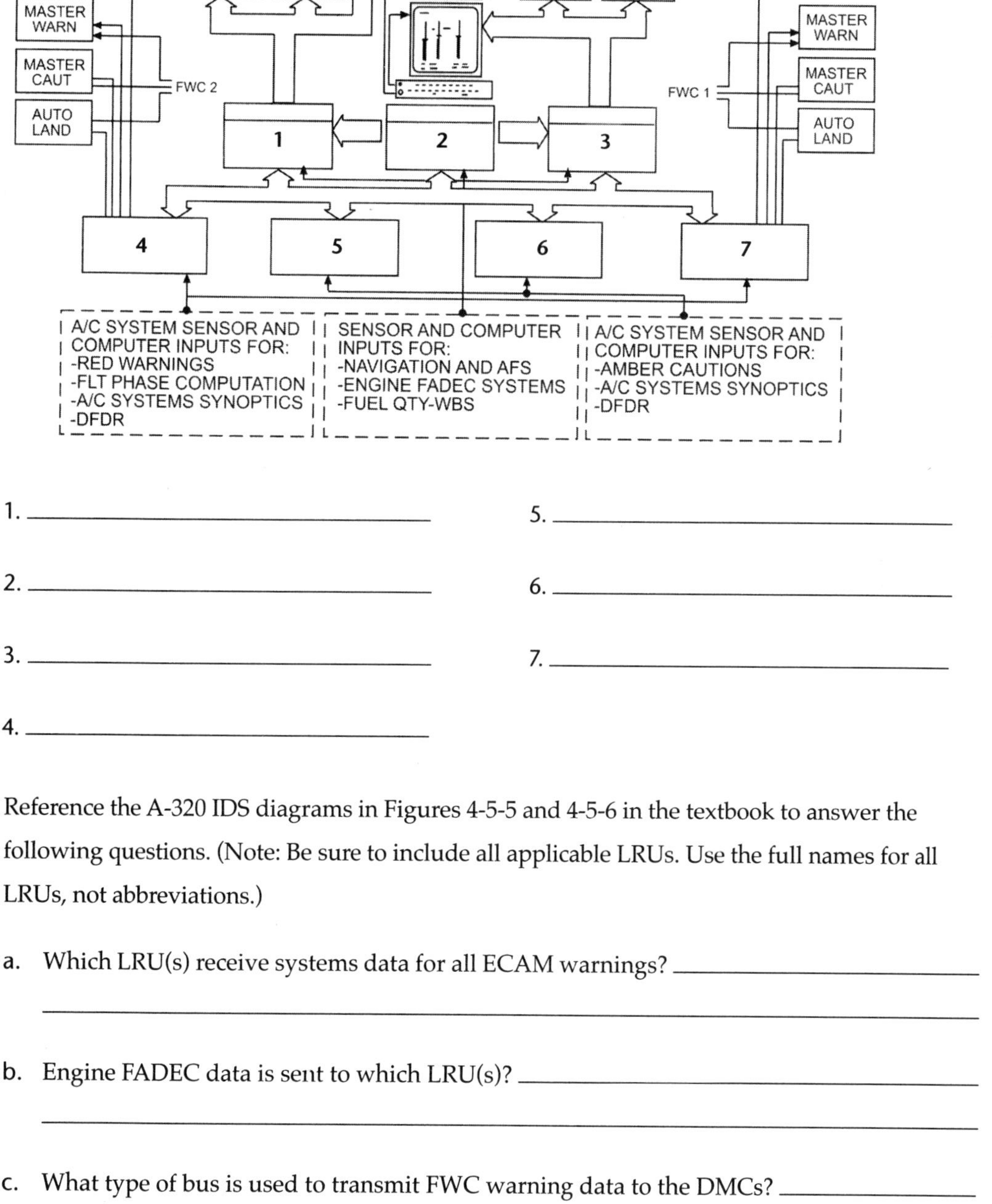

1. ______________________
2. ______________________
3. ______________________
4. ______________________
5. ______________________
6. ______________________
7. ______________________

11. Reference the A-320 IDS diagrams in Figures 4-5-5 and 4-5-6 in the textbook to answer the following questions. (Note: Be sure to include all applicable LRUs. Use the full names for all LRUs, not abbreviations.)

   a. Which LRU(s) receive systems data for all ECAM warnings? ______________________

   b. Engine FADEC data is sent to which LRU(s)? ______________________

   c. What type of bus is used to transmit FWC warning data to the DMCs? ______________________

   d. The master caution and warning lights receive data from which LRU(s)? ______________________

   e. What type of bus is used to transmit data from the display management computers to the display units? ______________________

Chapter 4: Integrated Monitoring and Warning Systems

ANALYSIS QUESTIONS

name:

date:

12. The A-320 employs several LRUs to operate the Electronic Centralized Aircraft Monitoring system. Refer to Figures 4-5-9 and 4-5-10 in the textbook to answer the following questions concerning the interface between these LRUs.

    a. What type of signals are used to transmit information from the aircraft systems to the System Data Acquisition Concentrators? Name all that apply. ________________

    b. What type of signals are used to transmit information from the aircraft systems to the Flight Warning Computers? Name all that apply. ________________

    c. What type of data is transmitted between the two Flight Warning Computers? ________________

    d. How many busses are used to transmit information from the System Data Acquisition Concentrators to the three Display Management Computers? ________________

13. The A-320 CFDS employs a series of classes and levels to determine the significance of a given system fault. Reference textbook Figure 4-5-21 to answer the following questions concerning A-320 system faults. (Note: Be sure to indicate ALL that apply.)

    a. Which fault recorded by ECAM is more serious: Class 1 or Class 3? ________________

    b. Which fault recorded by ECAM is more serious: Class 1, Level 3 or Class 1, Level 1? ________________

    c. What will occur during a Class 1, Level 2 fault: master warning light, master caution light, continuous repetitive chime, single chime, a recorded ECAM message, fault recorded by the Central Maintenance Computer, or failure indicated on ECAM status page under maintenance? Choose all that apply. ________________

    d. What will occur during a Class 2 fault?
    Circle all that apply:

    master warning light
    master caution light
    continuous repetitive chime
    single chime
    a recorded ECAM message
    fault recorded by the Central Maintenance Computer
    failure indicated only on ECAM status page under maintenance

Chapter 4:
Integrated Monitoring and Warning Systems

ANALYSIS QUESTIONS

name:

date:

14. Reference Figure 4-5-22 in the textbook to answer the following questions about the A-320 flight phases.

    a. When the aircraft reaches 80 knots at takeoff what ECAM system page is displayed? ________________________

    b. What system page is displayed when the aircraft descends to 800 feet? ________________________

    c. During flight phase six, what warnings does the ECAM inhibit? ________________________

    d. What flight condition marks the beginning and end of flight phase nine? ________________________

15. Insert the name of each LRU shown on the following of the B-787 instrument panel. Provide the acronym and the full name of the LRU.

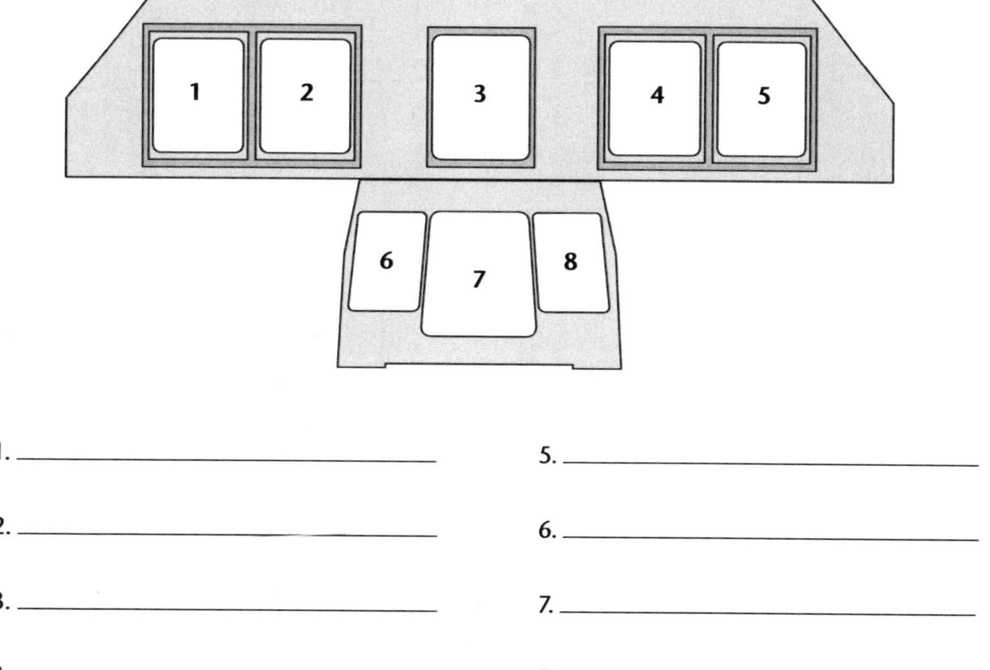

1. ________________________
2. ________________________
3. ________________________
4. ________________________
5. ________________________
6. ________________________
7. ________________________
8. ________________________

16. According to Figure 4-6-8 in the textbook, what LRUs are connected using the RS-485 data bus?

Chapter 4:

Integrated Monitoring and Warning Systems

17. According to Figure 4-6-10 of the textbook, how many high-speed data busses are used to connect each GIA to each PFD?

ANALYSIS QUESTIONS

18. According to the TCAS example in Figure 4-6-12 in the textbook, which aircraft will trigger a TCAS alarm because of a violation of DMOD minimums?

name:

date:

Chapter 5: Integrated Test Equipment

FILL IN THE BLANK QUESTIONS

name:

date:

1. BITE stands for ____________________.

2. The latest generation of built-in test equipment found on the Boeing 747-400 aircraft is called the ____________________.

3. A Boeing 757 or 767 aircraft utilizes built-in test equipment systems on approximately __________ LRUs located throughout the aircraft.

4. The Boeing 757 and 767 incorporate a maintenance control display unit to monitor and test the __________ computers, __________ computers, and the __________ computers.

5. The B-757 MCDU receives digital data in an __________ format transmitted from the thrust management, flight control, and flight management computers along with various other system inputs.

6. The B-747-400 CMCS is accessed through one of four __________.

7. The Collins EFIS-85B and -86B employ BITS mode to provide troubleshooting data stored the processors' __________.

8. The CMCs __________ function examines faults from previous flight legs and is used to aid in the troubleshooting and repair of chronic problems.

9. The B-747-400 CMC can store up to __________ fault messages in a nonvolatile memory.

10. The Central Maintenance Computers on the B-747-400 each have ten ARINC __________ output busses.

11. The __________ are push-button switches located on the perimeter of the control display units used to select items for display, or activate available functions.

12. Considering the B-747-400 CMCs, the present leg is defined as the elapsed time between __________ and __________.

13. Any EICAS message or parameter exceedance, any primary flight display (PFD) flag, or any navigational display (ND) flag is commonly referred to as a __________ effect.

14. The B-747-400 CMC menu contains seven available options from the CMC. These options are: (1) __________, (2) __________, (3) __________, (4) __________, (5) __________, (6) __________, (7) __________.

15. A __________ is considered any FDE or CMC message that is not caused by an actual fault.

Chapter 5: Integrated Test Equipment

FILL IN THE BLANK QUESTIONS

name:

date:

16. The B-747-400 CMCS report menu contains two options. These options are printer and ______________.

17. The B-747-400 CMCs ______________ function consists of any real time faults monitored by the CMC that are present at the time of CMCS interrogation.

18. The present leg is considered leg number 00; the fault previous to that is numbered flight leg ______________.

19. The ______________ function of the CMC is used to access real time data for 11 different aircraft systems.

20. The EICAS maintenance page data is displayed on the (Choose one: upper or lower) ______________ EICAS display.

21. The ______________ function of the CMCS allows for preflight testing of three aircraft systems: the stall warning/stick shaker, the take off configuration of the aircraft, and the ground proximity warning computer (GPWC).

22. On the B-747-400, the ______________ maintenance pages are used to access information on the integrated display system (IDS) software numbers and LRU pin programming.

23. The ______________ function of the CMCS is typically used to further define faults found during other CMC tests.

24. CMCs input monitoring function is used to display ______________ from various LRUs to the CMCs or EIUs.

25. The ______________ function of the CMC allows for verification of part numbers and programming options for the brake system control unit (BSCU) and the central maintenance computer (CMC).

26. Airbus's aircraft use the ______________ for fault isolation and system analysis.

27. In the Centralized Fault Display System (CFDS), there are three categories of type 1 systems. They are ______________, ______________, and ______________.

28. There are three system types that encompass all LRUs monitored by A-320 CFDS. The three classifications are ______________, ______________, and ______________.

29. On the A-320 CFDS, a Class ______________ failure will always display a discrete caution or warning annunciator.

Chapter 5: Integrated Test Equipment

FILL IN THE BLANK QUESTIONS

name:

date:

30. In the A-320 centralized fault display system there are five main functions of the CFDIU. These functions are: (1) ____________, (2) ____________, (3) ____________, (4) ____________, and (5) ____________.

31. The backup section of the CFDIU provides redundancy for two basic functions, the CFDS report/test function and the ____________.

32. Considering the A-320 CFDS, there are three main failure classifications: ____________, ____________, and ____________.

33. On the A-320, CFDS Class ____________ failures will have no message or status page information displayed on ECAM.

34. The in-flight mode of the CFDS allows the flight crew to access ____________ and ____________.

35. Using the on ground mode of the CFDS, the following six reports can be assessed: (1) ____________, (2) ____________, (3) ____________, (4) ____________, (5) ____________, and (6) ____________.

36. The two classifications of failures reported by the A-320 CFDS last legs reports are ____________ and ____________.

37. On the A-320, the previous legs report can store up to ____________ flight legs and a total of ____________ failures.

38. At the beginning of each new flight of the A-320 (start of the first engine), the last leg report currently in memory is transferred to the ____________ memory.

39. The CFDS ____________ data presents a list of systems that are affected by a current failure.

40. The CFDS ____________ function is used during ground operations only for an in-depth look at the faults that occurred in a particular system.

41. ____________ is a design concept that allows for advanced software technologies and improved data bus communications between aircraft systems.

42. Many new aircraft also utilize ____________ communication systems (local area network, satellite or airborne cell) for the download of system performance data.

43. The collection of data needed for maintenance analysis is often called ____________.

44. On the B-777, the central maintenance system data is accessed through the ____________.

Chapter 5: Integrated Test Equipment

FILL IN THE BLANK QUESTIONS

name:

date:

45. On the B-777, there are two AIMS cabinets; each of the cabinets contains ________________ (insert number) line replaceable modules (LRMs).

46. The A-380 ________________________________ is designed to manage all data related to system configuration including all data uploads/downloads.

47. The A-380 ________________________________ can transmit trend data to ground facilities for real time analysis during flight; or the data can be downloaded after landing.

48. The Boeing 787 Central Maintenance Computer System will employ an integrated architecture using an ARINC ____________ (insert number) data bus structure.

49. The Honeywell ____________ 2000 system is an integrated avionics suite installed on many modern corporate and commuter-type aircraft.

50. In general, the Primus ____________ will monitor functional performance of both hardware and software during four distinct phases of operation; power-up, continuous monitoring, pilot activated and ground maintenance tests.

51. The Phenom has the capability to employ ________________ connectivity for the download/upload of data.

Chapter 5: Integrated Test Equipment

MULTIPLE CHOICE QUESTIONS

name:

date:

1. What are self-contained diagnostic systems found on modern aircraft often called?
   a. BITS
   b. BUSS
   c. BITE
   d. BIDE

2. The B-757 contains several systems that employ BITE. Which of the following is true of this type of BITE?
   a. The BITE data is accessed through a given LRU using an LED display.
   b. The BITE data is accessed from the flight deck using a carry-on analyzer.
   c. The BITE data is displayed on the lower EICAS display when requested for maintenance.
   d. The BITE data is displayed by EICAS only with the aircraft on the ground and the parking brake set.

3. The Boeing 757 and 767 incorporate a Maintenance Control Display Unit (MCDU) to monitor and test various systems. Which of the following statement(s) is/are true concerning the MCDU?
   a. The MCDU can be accessed from the electrical equipment bay or the flight deck using a carry-on unit.
   b. The MCDU monitors the flight control computers, flight management computers, and the thrust management computers.
   c. The MCDU can store fault data for up to ten previous flights.
   d. All of the above.

4. The BITS mode fault diagnostics program is found on which of the following systems?
   a. All transport category aircraft that use Honeywell flight management systems.
   b. Transport category aircraft that employ central maintenance computers
   c. Early version transport category aircraft like the B-727.
   d. Corporate aircraft that employ Collins Electronic Flight Instrument Systems (EFIS).

5. Where is the fault data accessed for the B-747-400 Central Maintenance Computer System?
   a. The fault data is accessed through one of four CDUs.
   b. The fault data is accessed through a printer in the electrical equipment bay.
   c. The fault data is accessed through a 24-character LED display on the MCDU.
   d. The fault data is accessed through the main EICAS display.

6. What system is used on the B-747-400 for fault monitoring and isolation?
   a. Central Maintenance Computer System
   b. Centralized Fault Display System
   c. Engine Indicating and Crew Alerting System
   d. Airplane Information Management System

7. How many Central Maintenance Computers (CMCs) are used in the B-747-400 CMC System?
   a. One
   b. Two
   c. Three
   d. Four

8. Which of the following statements is true concerning the Line Select Keys (LSK) found on the B-747-400?
   a. The LSKs are used to select items for display or activate functions available on the CDU.
   b. The LSKs are found on the perimeter of the main EICAS display.
   c. The LSKs are used to unlock the central maintenance system once the aircraft is on the ground.
   d. The LSKs are part of the Electronic Instrument System (EIS) and used to select what items will be displayed on the primary Flight Displays (PFD) and Navigational Displays (ND).

9. What are the two basic formats presented under the present faults function of the B-747-400 CMCs?
   a. ECAM faults and CMC messages
   b. EICAS faults and present leg messages
   c. Present leg faults and present leg messages
   d. CMC faults and present leg messages

Chapter 5: Integrated Test Equipment

MULTIPLE CHOICE QUESTIONS

name:

date:

10. On the B-747-400 Central Maintenance Computer System the term Present Leg is defined as which of the following?
    a. The Present Leg begins when the landing gear are raised and ends when the landing gear are lowered.
    b. The Present Leg is defined as the first flight of each calendar day.
    c. The Present Leg is defined as the elapsed time between first engine start and last engine shut down.
    d. The Present Leg is defined as the elapsed time between take off and touchdown.

11. A flight deck effect can be defined as which of the following?
    a. Any EICAS (or ECAM) message or parameter exceedance, any primary flight display (PFD) flag, or any navigational display (ND) flag.
    b. Any indication on the control display unit related to a flight fault
    c. All flight or ground faults recorded by the central maintenance computer.
    d. All flight or ground faults not recorded by the central maintenance computer but displayed by EICAS.

12. What manual is used in conjunction with CMCS message data for troubleshooting the B-747-400?
    a. Fault Isolation Manual
    b. EICAS Message Manual
    c. Fault Code Index Manual
    d. CMC Message Manual

13. What function of the software program is used by the Boeing 747-400 CMCS to help eliminate nuisance messages?
    a. Fault phase screening
    b. Fault history screening
    c. Flight faulty screening
    d. Flight phase screening

14. The B-747-400 Central Maintenance Computers can record how many different flight phases?
    a. 2
    b. 4
    c. 14
    d. 24

15. What parameter is recorded by the CMC to indicate the airplane's configuration at the time a system failed?
    a. The flight phase when the fault occurred
    b. The speed of the aircraft when the fault occurred
    c. All flight deck effects at the time the fault occurred
    d. All EICAS manual events recorded when the fault occurred

16. Generally speaking, what is a nuisance message displayed by an aircraft's central maintenance system?
    a. Any flight deck effect or fault message that is not correlated to a pilot's log entry.
    b. Any fault data that does not provide an ATA maintenance manual code.
    c. Any fault data or flight deck effect that is not caused by an actual fault.
    d. Any fault data that does not affect flight safety.

17. How many flight legs can be stored in the B-747-400 CMCS fault history?
    a. 10
    b. 99
    c. 256
    d. 500

18. On the B-747-400, the EICAS maintenance pages present which of the following types of data?
    a. EICAS faults and CMC fault messages
    b. Flight management system fault data
    c. Real time data, auto event data, manual event data
    d. 32-bit ARINC 429 data

Chapter 5: Integrated Test Equipment

MULTIPLE CHOICE QUESTIONS

name:

date:

19. The confidence tests function of the B-747-400 CMCS is often used for which of the following?
    a. Preflight testing of three vital aircraft systems.
    b. Tests during routine maintenance of the EIS.
    c. Troubleshooting last leg faults.
    d. Troubleshooting the central maintenance computer system.

20. Which of the following is a section of a typical Fault Isolation Manual that would be used during fault isolation?
    a. EICAS messages
    b. Fault code index
    c. CMCS message index
    d. All of the above

21. If a technician is unable to repair an aircraft system, what manual must be referenced to determine if the aircraft can return to service?
    a. The aircraft's flight manual
    b. The aircraft's troubleshooting manual
    c. The aircraft's dispatch handbook
    d. The aircraft's minimum equipment list

22. What function of the B-747-400 CMCS is used to access real time ARINC 429 data in a 32-bit format?
    a. Configuration tests
    b. Input monitoring
    c. Shop faults
    d. Confidence tests

23. What is the name for the advanced diagnostics and fault isolation system used on Airbus aircraft?
    a. Central Maintenance Computer System
    b. Centralized Fault Display System
    c. Built-in Test Equipment
    d. Electronic Centralized Aircraft Monitor

24. What system can be used to transmit information directly from the aircraft's centralized fault computers to the airline ground facilities?
    a. The Number 1 VHF Communications Transceiver
    b. The Flight Warning Computer (FWC)
    c. The Airborne Communication Addressing and Reporting System (ACARS)
    d. The Maintenance Control Display Unit (MCDU)

25. On the A-320 how many Centralized Fault Display Interface Units (CFDIU) are employed in the Centralized Fault Display System (CFDS)?
    a. 1
    b. 2
    c. 3
    d. 4

26. Concerning the A-320, which class of failure will have the most serious consequences on aircraft performance?
    a. Class I
    b. Class II
    c. Class III
    d. Class IV

27. On the A-320, what two CFDs reports can be accessed during flight?
    a. Current leg reports and current leg ECAM reports
    b. Present leg reports and present leg ECAM reports
    c. Previous leg reports and previous leg ECAM reports
    d. Recent leg reports and recent leg ECAM reports

Chapter 5: Integrated Test Equipment

MULTIPLE CHOICE QUESTIONS

name:

date:

28. Which LRU is used by the A-320 to access fault data from the CFDS?
    a. The Multipurpose Control and Display Unit (MCDU)
    b. The Multifunctional Display Unit (MDU)
    c. The Control Display Unit (CDU)
    d. The Centralized Fault Display Unit (CFDU)

29. The CFDS avionics status data is available on which of the following aircraft?
    a. B-757
    b. B-767
    c. B-747-400
    d. A-320

30. On the A-320, what level of troubleshooting involves an in-depth study of the failed system through access of the binary or hexadecimal fault code data?
    a. Level 1
    b. Level 2
    c. Level 3
    d. Level 4

31. What system employs line replaceable modules (LRM) on the Boeing 777 to integrate a multitude of electronic systems?
    a. AIMS
    b. ECAS
    c. EFIS
    d. ECAM

32. Which of the following best describes where an aircraft can download data using a wireless hot spot at a typical airport?
    a. Within 100 yards, directly in front of the airplane's maintenance facility
    b. At the end of each runway and in front of the terminal gates
    c. Coverage is available throughout the entire airport
    d. Only inside a maintenance hanger

33. Which classification is used by the Primus Built-In Test Equipment (BITE) to indicate a fault that is stored in the BITE memory and only available for maintenance activities?
    a. Critical
    b. Noncritical
    c. Status
    d. Maintenance

34. What Primus BITE classification is used to indicate a system fault that would effect primary aircraft functions?
    a. Maintenance
    b. Level 1
    c. Level 2
    d. Critical

Chapter 5: Integrated Test Equipment

ANALYSIS QUESTIONS

name:

date:

1. Study the Radio Altimeter BITE test procedures listed in Figure 5-2-4 in the textbook then answer then following questions.

   a. What should be displayed on the captain's EADI radio altimeter indication while the RA R/T test switch is depressed?__________

   b. What should be displayed on the captain's EADI radio altimeter indication when the RA R/T test switch is released? __________

   c. What is detected if the red antenna (ANT) LED illuminates while the RA R/T test switch is depressed? __________

2. Study the Boeing 747-400 CMCS system architecture and answer the following questions. Refer to textbook Figure 5-3-3 and related readings.

   a. Which LRU(s) send digital data to the CMCS data loader? __________

   b. What type of data is output from the data loader to the CMCs? Identify the specific digital signal format. __________

   c. Which LRU(s) send data through the switching module to the data loader? __________

   d. The printer sends data to which LRU(s)? __________

3. Complete the following table according to the B-747-400 CMCS interface connections outlined in Tables 5-3-1, 5-3-2, and 5-3-3 in the textbook.

LRU	ARINC OUTPUT BUS FROM CMC (LIST BUS NUMBER)	DISCRETE OUTPUT FROM CMC TO LRU (YES OR NO)	DISCRETE INPUT TO CMC FROM LRU (YES OR NO)
Left Flight Control Computer			
Right Flight Control Computer			
Center Flight Control Computer			
Left Radio Communications Panel			
R7421, Left Pitot Probe Test Relay			

Chapter 5: Integrated Test Equipment

ANALYSIS QUESTIONS

name:

date:

4. Power for the B-747-400 central maintenance computers comes from several sources. Answer the following questions according to the CMC power and switching relay schematics in textbook Figures 5-3-5 and 5-3-6 and related readings.

   a. What is the function of the ground test enable relays? ______

   b. What voltage is used to power the CMC enable relays? Provide voltage value and units. ______

   c. What bus supplies voltage to the eight CMC ground test enable relays? ______

   d. On what panel is the circuit breaker located for the eight CMC ground test enable relays? ______

   e. What voltage is used to power the left CMC? Provide voltage value and units. ______

   f. What bus supplies voltage to the left CMC? ______

   g. On what panel is the circuit breaker located for the left CMC? ______

   h. When the remote ground test switch (S2090) is in the normal position, are the enable relays energized, yes or no? ______

   i. When the ground test switch (S2089) is in the enable position, are the EIUs grounded through Enable Relay 6, yes or no? ______

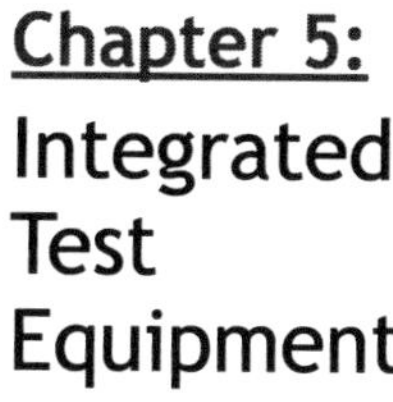

5. The Present Leg Faults display for a Boeing 747-400 is used to review faults from the most recent flight leg. Describe the type of information presented by the CMC Present Leg Faults display in the following diagram. Record your answer on the lines provided.

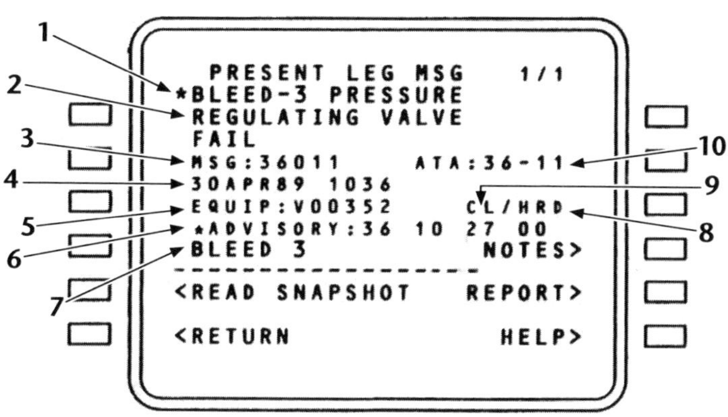

ANALYSIS QUESTIONS

name:

date:

1. ____________________
2. ____________________
3. ____________________
4. ____________________
5. ____________________
6. ____________________
7. ____________________
8. ____________________
9. ____________________
10. ____________________

6. The B-747-400 has the capability to print various types of CMCS reports. Answer the following questions according to the CMC printout shown in Figure 5-3-11 in the textbook.

   a. Is the fault IRU-C FAIL an intermittent or hard failure? ____________________

   b. What is the registration (N number) of the aircraft from which this report is taken? ____________________

   c. What is the ATA chapter and section for the wiring diagram needed to repair the fault in the failed right FCC? ____________________

   d. What is the CMCS message number for the failed right IRU? ____________________

   e. Is the failed C-IRU fault still active? ____________________

   f. At what time of day did the left FMC fail? Show units in GMT. ____________________

   g. What flight phase was the aircraft in when the right IRU failed? ____________________

Chapter 5: Integrated Test Equipment

ANALYSIS QUESTIONS

name:

date:

7. Referring to textbook Figure 5-3-14, answer the following questions as they relate to the B-747-400 Central Maintenance Computer System Fault History Message page.

   a. During which flight leg(s) did the No. 3 bleed air pressure regulating valve experience a hard failure? __________

   b. During which flight leg(s) did the No. 3 bleed air pressure regulating valve experience an intermittent failure? __________

   c. In what ATA chapter and section number would information be found on this fault?

      ____

   d. What type of fault message was displayed on EICAS related to the No. 3 bleed air pressure regulating valve fault, warning, caution, advisory, or memo? __________

      ____

   e. What is the CMCS message number for the No. 3 bleed air pressure regulating valve fault?

      ____

8. The Configuration function of the B-747-400 Central Maintenance Computer System allows for verification of certain part numbers and program pins. Answer the following questions concerning the Configuration Page shown in Figure 5-3-23 in the textbook.

   a. What are the two airline option codes for the left CMC? __________
      and __________

   b. What is the software configuration number for the left CMC? __________

   c. The configuration option is found under which function of the CMC menu? On which page of the menu is it found? __________

   d. Configuration data is available for which two systems? __________
      and __________

Chapter 5: Integrated Test Equipment

ANALYSIS QUESTIONS

name:

date:

9. The Boeing 747-400 Fault Isolation Manual (FIM) is used during initial system troubleshooting. Answer the following questions according to pages from the FIM shown in Figures 5-3-24, 5-3-25, and 5-3-26 in the textbook.

   a. According to fault code 24 11 02 00 what are the possible CMC message numbers? ______

   b. What ATA spec 100 chapter and subject apply to the fault code 24 11 02 00? ______

   c. Which figure shows the manual page needed to find a fault code from an EICAS message?

   d. Which figure shows the flight crew's log entry that does not relate to a specific fault code?

10. Answer the following questions according to 24-31-06 page 501 from the B-747-400 maintenance manual. Reference textbook Figure 5-3-35.

    a. What is the ATA iSpecification 2200 number for the APU battery wiring diagram? ______

    b. Where is the APU battery located? Provide a general location and specific equipment rack number. ______

    c. What page of the aircraft maintenance manual is used to provide instructions for removal of electrical power? Give complete ATA code and page numbers. ______

11. The A-320 CFDIU uses two types of data to request and transmit BITE information: discrete data signals and digital data signal. Answer the following questions on the A-320 CFDS according to textbook Figures 5-4-4 and 5-4-5.

    a. What type of signal is transmitted from the Centralized Fault Display Interface Unit to type three systems? ______

    b. What type of signal is transmitted from the type three system BITE to the CFDIU? ______

    c. What type of signal is transmitted from the Centralized Fault Display Interface Unit to type one systems? ______

    d. What type of signal is transmitted from the type one system BITE to the CFDIU? ______

Chapter 5:
Integrated Test Equipment

ANALYSIS QUESTIONS

name:

date:

12. The A-320 CFDIU receives data from a variety of LRUs. Answer the following questions concerning CFDIU data according to textbook Figure 5-4-7. Use full names for all LRUs, not the acronym.

    a. Which LRU transmits flight number and city pair data to the CFDIU? ____________________

    ____

    b. Which LRUs receive city pair data from the CFDIU? ____________________

    ____

    c. Which LRU transmits all ECAM warnings to the CFDIU? ____________________

    ____

13. The following diagram is a typical Last Leg Report from an A-320 CFDS. Record a description of the data on the lines provided.

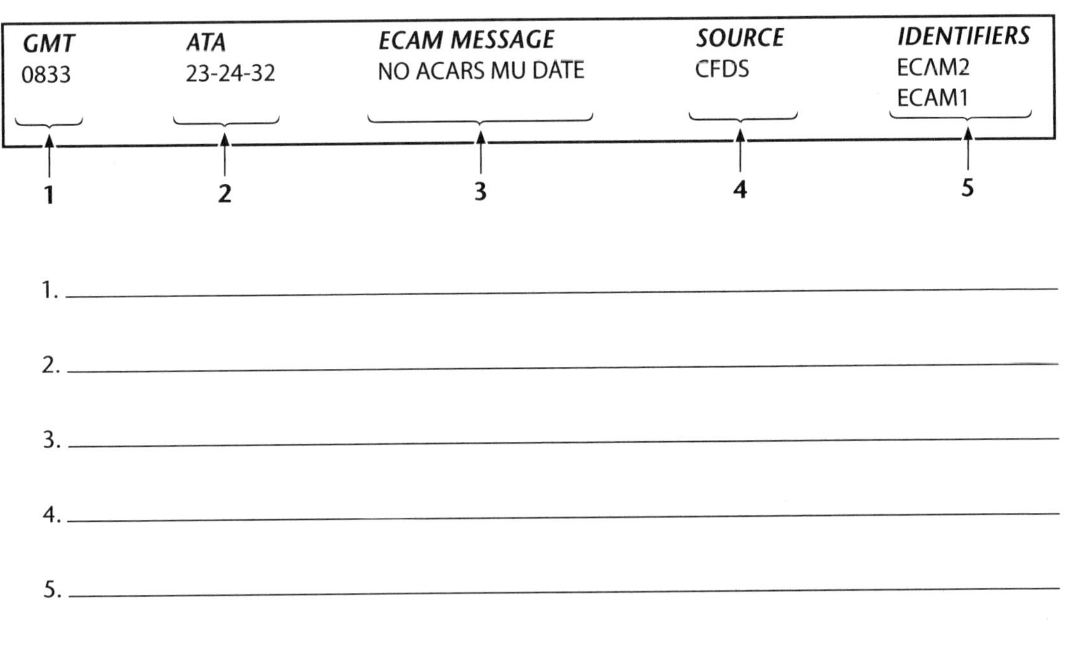

1. ____
2. ____
3. ____
4. ____
5. ____

____

14. Level three troubleshooting on the A-320 requires an analysis of binary digits. Use Figure 5-4-23 and Table 5-4-2 in the textbook to decode ATA from the bleed air monitor computer label 066.

    a. What is the position of the No. 2 engine OPV? ____________________

    b. What is the position of the No. 2 engine FAV? (Hint: Two separate bits define this position)

    ____

    c. Is there a No. 2 engine bleed fault? ____________________

Chapter 5: Integrated Test Equipment

ANALYSIS QUESTIONS

name:

date:

15. Using CFDS information and various A-320 manuals, the technician can find information to repair a system fault or defer the repair until the next maintenance opportunity. Use Figures 5-4-27 through 5-4-33 in the textbook to answer the following questions concerning system repair.

    a. According the crew log entry, where was the fault message ENG 2 FADEC A displayed?

    ____

    b. At what time did the ECAM message ENG 2 FADEC A appear? ______________________________

    c. What was the aircraft's registration number that experienced the fault ENG 2 FADEC A?

    ____

    d. What was the fault message recorded by the CFDS from FWC1 for the ECAM message ENG 2 FADEC A? ______________________________

    e. What must be done to defer this repair until the next maintenance opportunity? __________

    ____

    f. To repair this fault, what fault isolation procedure task number would be referenced?

    ____

    g. To remove the EEC, what maintenance manual would be referenced? Supply the ATA specification 2200 six-digit number. ______________________________

16. List the four functions integrated by the B-777 Airplane Information Management System (AIMS).

17. List two LRUs through which a technician can access the A-380 Central Maintenance System (CMS).

Chapter 5:
Integrated Test Equipment

ANALYSIS QUESTIONS

name:

date:

18. On the blanks below, write the name of each numbered LRU (1-7) pictured on this diagram of the Honeywell Primus system.

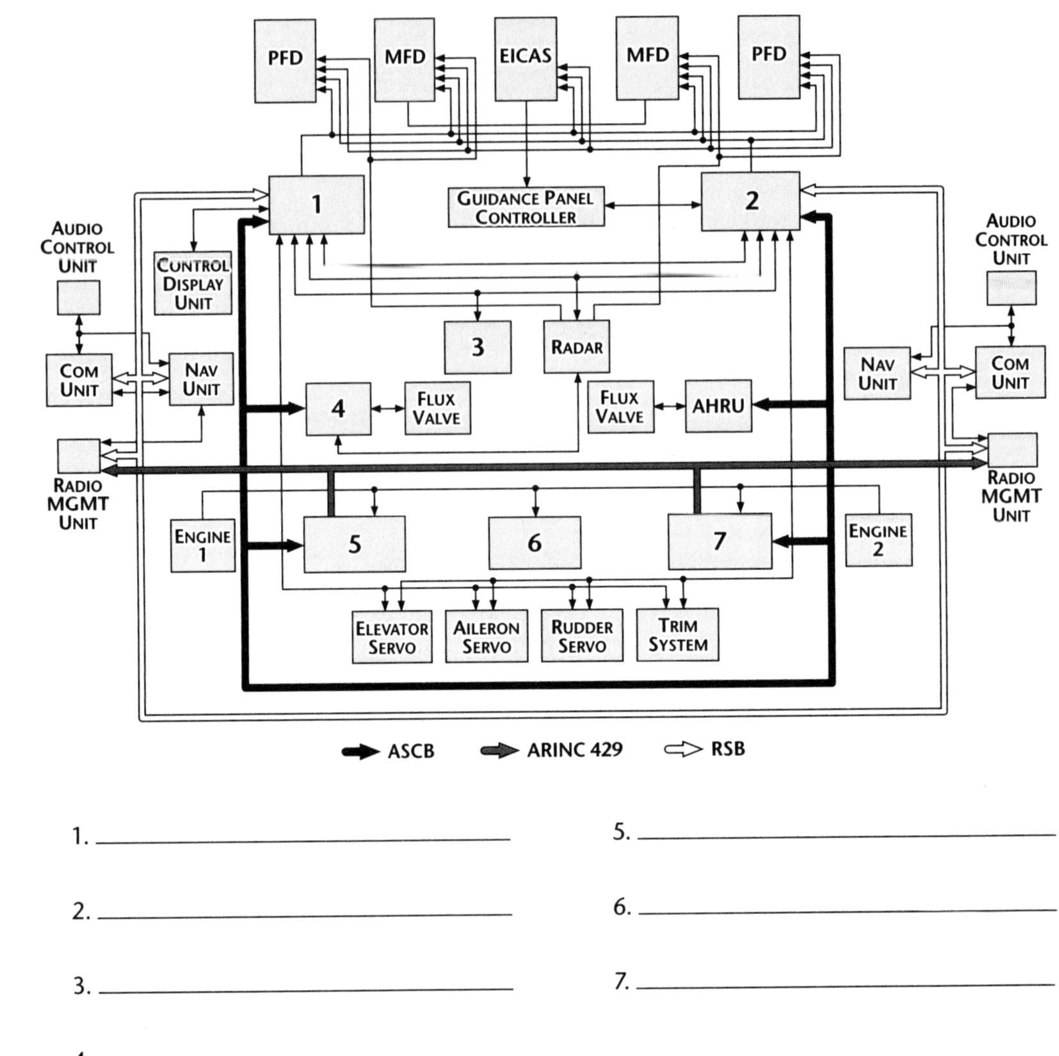

1. ______________________________

2. ______________________________

3. ______________________________

4. ______________________________

5. ______________________________

6. ______________________________

7. ______________________________

19. List the three classifications used by the Primus Built-In Test Equipment (BITE).

Chapter 6: Autopilot and Autoflight Systems

FILL IN THE BLANK QUESTIONS

name:

date:

1. Simple autopilots provide guidance for only the longitudinal axis of the aircraft. These systems, often found on light single engine aircraft, are called ______________________ because they are used to keep the wings level.

2. A ______________________ is used to inform the autopilot computer that the control surface has changed position. This system allows the computer to anticipate when the control surfaces should be returned to the neutral position.

3. The ______________________ allows the autopilot to fly the selected lateral navigational course (i.e. control of north, south, east, and west directions). The ______________________ allows the autopilot to fly the selected altitude or glide path.

4. The aerodynamics of a swept back wing causes a stability problem known as ______________________ .

5. The two common types of gyroscopic sensors used in modern autopilots are ______________________ and ______________________ .

6. Rotating mass gyros are often used to stabilize acceleration sensors mounted on ______________________ .

7. The ______________________ is an angular rate sensor and performs the same function as a rotating mass gyro using no moving parts.

8. The term ______________________ stands for light amplification by stimulated emission of radiation.

9. An ______________________ is a device that senses aircraft acceleration. It should be noted that acceleration is a ______________________ force and therefore is measured in both magnitude and direction.

10. Modern accelerometers are often small ______________________ systems (MEMS), consisting of little more than a ______________________ with a small mass at the end.

11. On many transport category aircraft, there are at least ______________ accelerometers to monitor the acceleration of each aircraft axis.

12. The three elements typically measured by an air data system are ______________________, ______________________ pressure and ______________________ pressure .

13. ______________________ pressure is the absolute pressure of the air that surrounds the aircraft, which varies inversely with the altitude of the aircraft and also changes with the general atmospheric conditions of the area.

14. ______________________ is an absolute pressure of the air that is "pressed" into the front of the aircraft. With the aircraft at rest this pressure is equal to static pressure.

Chapter 6: Autopilot and Autoflight Systems

FILL IN THE BLANK QUESTIONS

name:

date:

15. The difference between pitot pressure and static pressure is often referred to as ______________________ and is used to determine the aircraft's airspeed.

16. The three most common types of air data systems are the ______________________, ______________________, and ______________________ systems.

17. An ______________________ system monitors pitot pressure, static pressure and air temperature to determine various parameters, such as airspeed, altitude, and vertical climb.

18. The ______________________ compass system employs one or more remote sensors to produce an electric signal that can be used to determine the aircraft's position relative to magnetic North.

19. The remote sensor used in a flux gate compass system is called a ______________________ or ______________________.

20. An Air Data Inertial Reference Unit combines air data sensors and the components of a typical IRU to provide a variety of critical flight data such as ______________________ and ______________________ information.

21. An ______________________ is a combination of laser gyros and accelerometers used to sense the aircraft's angular rates and accelerations.

22. During initialization, the IRS accelerometers measure the direction of the earth's gravity force to determine the aircraft's ______________________, which is a direction perpendicular to the rotational axis of the earth that intersects the aircraft's position.

23. A servo is a device used to apply a force to the aircraft's control surface in response to an autopilot command. The three basic types of servos are pneumatic, ______________________, and ______________________.

24. The ______________________ servo is a vacuum actuated unit used on simple autopilots for light aircraft.

25. ______________________ servos utilize an electric motor and clutch assembly to move the aircraft's control surface according to autopilot commands.

26. ______________________ servos are the most powerful type of servo actuator; therefore, these units are typically used on transport category aircraft.

27. The two most common devices used to generate the feedback signal are the ______________________ and the ______________________.

28. Two common types of transducers used for autopilot feedback systems are the ______________ and the ______________ (insert acronyms).

Chapter 6:
Autopilot and Autoflight Systems

FILL IN THE BLANK QUESTIONS

name:

date:

29. Tachometer generators (or tach generators) are often used in electric servo systems as ________________________ .

30. The AHC contains a dual sensor assembly that houses two rotating wheels mounted at 90 degree angles from each other. The spinning wheels, which rotate at a constant 2,500 r.p.m., contain four piezoelectric crystals called ____________________ .

31. The three modes in which the APS-85 diagnostics operate are the input, __________________, and ____________________ modes.

32. Many autopilot problems come from the subsystems that feed the autopilot computer. One of the most complex and frequently failed subsystems is the __________________________.

33. The Embraer Phenom employs an avionics package constructed by _______________________ International.

34. The Embraer Phenom flight director employs _______________ (insert number) independent systems each located in number 1 and 2 GIA.

35. The Embraer Phenom employs a brake-by-wire system activated through the traditional flight deck __________________________ .

36. The B-747-400 Inertial Reference System (IRS) is used to provide ____________________ and _____________________ navigation, attitude information, acceleration, and speed data to a variety of aircraft systems.

37. The B-747-400 ______________________________ is a computer-based system that reduces pilot workload by providing automatic radio tuning, lateral and vertical navigation, thrust management, and the display of flight plan maps.

38. The B-747-400 contains three ______________________________, which are used to enter data into the FMS.

39. The B-747-400 flight management computers (FMCs) are located in the main _________________________ .

40. The B-747-400 has three ______________________________, which are used by the autoflight system to interpret data and provide the necessary calculations for the autopilot and flight director functions.

41. The FMC sends output data to the ______________________________, which provide the control signals to the autothrottle servomotor.

42. The FMC output signals known as ______________________________ provide fine thrust adjustments that precisely equalize the thrust of all four engines.

Chapter 6: Autopilot and Autoflight Systems

FILL IN THE BLANK QUESTIONS

name:

date:

43. The B-747-400 ______________________ panel is the main interface between the flight crew and the AFCS.

44. The FCCs communicate to each other via a ______________________ data bus for exchange of health monitoring, and to provide redundancy for servo engage data.

45. Fly-by-wire systems employ ______________________ system to provide a "realistic feel" to the pilot through the flight deck controls.

46. On the B-777 the ______________________ are used to increase aircraft lift during takeoff and landing.

47. Modern ______________________ aircraft require a complex flight control system which employs several computers, digital data transfer, and multiple actuators for dozens of flight controls.

48. The Boeing ______________ was the first transport category aircraft designed to incorporate a fly-by-wire primary flight control system.

49. ______________________ protection is used to ensure the aircraft never exceeds the operational limits and enters into an unsafe configuration, such as a stall condition.

50. The Primary Flight Computers (PFC) are non-operational in the ______________ mode.

51. The B-777 ______________________ can control the aircraft on its selected vertical and horizontal flight path and selected airspeed.

52. The B-777 Thrust Management Computing Function (TMCF) is software used to send auto throttle commands to the throttle ______________________ and engine trim commands to the ______________________.

53. The A-380 primary flight control system employs three primary computers (PRIMs) which provide flight control, flight guidance and ______________________ functions.

Chapter 6: Autopilot and Autoflight Systems

MULTIPLE CHOICE QUESTIONS

name:

date:

1. A gimbal platform is used on many autoflight systems to stabilize the accelerometers. The gimbal platform is designed to:
   a. Always be aligned with the longitudinal axis of the aircraft.
   b. Provide a feedback signal with respect to control surface travel.
   c. Work only with laser gyros and digital systems.
   d. Remain parallel to the earth's surface.

2. The ring laser gyro determines the aircraft's angular displacement by measuring which of the following?
   a. The difference in light intensity between two laser beams
   b. The frequency shift between two laser beams
   c. The difference in light intensity between three laser beams
   d. The frequency shift between three laser beams

3. The terms pneumatic, electro-pneumatic and electronic air data are used to describe which of the following systems?
   a. An air data system
   b. An attitude heading system
   c. An autoflight system
   d. An engine autothrottle system

4. Which of the following statements is true concerning static air pressure?
   a. Static air pressure varies inversely with aircraft altitude.
   b. Static air pressure varies directly with the aircraft altitude.
   c. Static pressure is constant regardless of aircraft altitude.
   d. Static pressure increases with aircraft speed.

5. What type of air data system employs an air data computer and is typically employed in modern corporate and transport category aircraft?
   a. Electropneumatic system
   b. Electrodynamic systems
   c. Electronic systems
   d. Dynamic pneumatic systems

6. What is the name for the air pressure measured as it is compressed by the moving aircraft?
   a. True air pressure
   b. Static air pressure
   c. Density air pressure
   d. Pitot pressure

7. Which LRU is used to calculate airspeed, vertical climb, and altitude?
   a. The air data computer
   b. The flight control computer
   c. The electronic instrument system computer
   d. The air coupler computer

8. How many flux detectors would be installed on a typical corporate aircraft such as the Beechcraft King Air, and where would they be located?
   a. There are three flux detectors installed in the electrical equipment rack of the aircraft.
   b. There is three flux detectors; one installed in the magnetic compass and one installed in each wing tip.
   c. There are two flux detectors, one installed in each wing tip.
   d. There are two flux detectors installed in tail of the aircraft.

9. Which of the following best describes the basic operation of a flux detector (flux valve)?
   a. The operation of the flux detector relies on the interaction of the earth's magnetic field and the magnetic field induced in the flux frame by the 400 Hz excitation coil.
   b. The flux detector employs a pick-off units and a torque motor to keep the detector unit aligned with the aircraft. This ensures accurate heading measurements at any aircraft attitude.
   c. The flux detector uses rate sensors to detect aircraft motion; the motion data is processed and magnetic heading is determined.
   d. The flux detector employs accelerometers and processor circuitry that are used to calculate the difference between magnetic heading and true heading.

Chapter 6: Autopilot and Autoflight Systems

MULTIPLE CHOICE QUESTIONS

name:

date:

10. On the Embraer Phenom what type of data bus format is used to send data packets to the flight control servos?
    a. RS-485
    b. RS-232
    c. ARINC 429
    d. Ethernet

11. An Inertial Reference System (IRS) is often employed on modern complex aircraft as part of the autoflight system. What two subsystems are the major elements of a typical IRS?
    a. Laser gyros and accelerometers
    b. Flux valves and accelerometers
    c. Accelerometers and gimbal platforms
    d. Air data computers and laser gyros

12. An Inertial Reference System must go through a start-up procedure to establish an initial reference point. Which of the following statements is true concerning this start-up process?
    a. The start-up process is called local vertical and is performed with the aircraft motionless.
    b. The start-up procedure is called local vertical and must be performed with the aircraft aligned with the runway prior to take off.
    c. The start-up process is called initialization and is performed during the first five minutes of each flight.
    d. The start-up process is called initialization and is performed with the aircraft motionless.

13. How many laser gyros are contained in a typical Inertial Reference Unit (IRU)?
    a. None
    b. One
    c. Two
    d. Three

14. Pneumatic servos would typically be found on what type of aircraft?
    a. Light single engine aircraft
    b. Transport category aircraft
    c. Corporate turboprop aircraft
    d. Pneumatic servos are not used on aircraft

15. What is the name of the LRU used to move flight control surfaces in accordance with autopilot command signals?
    a. Tach generator
    b. Yaw damper
    c. Electric servo
    d. Gimbal actuator

16. What is the purpose of the clutch mechanism found on control surface servos?
    a. To disengage when the control surface reaches its limit of travel.
    b. To allow for a gentle movement of the control surface during autopilot engage.
    c. To lock the control surface in position according to autopilot commands.
    d. To allow the pilot to manually override the servo.

17. Which aircraft employs hybrid servos that combine hydraulic actuators and electric drive motors?
    a. B-777
    b. B-787
    c. A-380
    d. Both B and C

18. What are the two common systems used to generate a feedback signal that informs the autopilot of control surface movement?
    a. AC synchros and differential transducers
    b. Servo transducers and differential transducers
    c. Linear transducers and rotary transducers
    d. DC synchros and differential transducers

Chapter 6: Autopilot and Autoflight Systems

MULTIPLE CHOICE QUESTIONS

name:

date:

19. What device is most likely used to measure the rotational position of an aircraft control surface?
    a. An LVDT
    b. A flux detector
    c. A gimbal
    d. An RVDT

20. Which of the following statements is true concerning differential traducers?
    a. Differential transducers are transistorized sensors used to measure aircraft acceleration.
    b. Differential transducers are typically used in conjunction with pneumatic servos.
    c. Differential transducers produce a digital output signal.
    d. Differential transducers are a mutual inductive device with a primary winding and two secondary windings.

21. How is the output signal changed as the rotary voltage differential transducer changes direction of travel?
    a. The AC signal changes phase
    b. The digital output changes from binary one to binary zero
    c. The output voltage changes
    d. The output current changes

22. What type of aircraft would typically employ the Collins APS-85 autopilot system?
    a. Light single engine aircraft
    b. Corporate aircraft
    c. Modern transport category aircraft
    d. Older transport category aircraft

23. Which of the following units is typically used to measure the rotational speed of an electric servomotor and provide feedback to the autopilot computer?
    a. LVDT
    b. Accelerometer
    c. Tach generator
    d. AC synchro

24. How many channels are used by the Flight Control Computer (FCC) on the APS-85 autopilot?
    a. One
    b. Two
    c. Three
    d. Four

25. The Attitude Heading Computer (AHC) in the Collins AHS-85 measures angular rates and accelerations using which of the following?
    a. Piezoelectric sensors
    b. Laser gyros
    c. LVDTs and RVDTs
    d. Tach generators

26. Which of the following statements is true concerning flight director systems?
    a. The flight director indicator can be displayed by EFIS.
    b. The flight director and autopilot functions are typically isolated when the autopilot is engaged.
    c. The flight director indications are often controlled through the autopilot computer.
    d. All of the above

27. How often must a pitot/static leak test be performed according to FAR 91.411 Part 43, Appendix E?
    a. Every 12 months
    b. Every annual inspection
    c. During major overhaul of the aircraft
    d. Every 24 months

Chapter 6: Autopilot and Autoflight Systems

MULTIPLE CHOICE QUESTIONS

name:

date:

28. On the Embraer Phenom aircraft how often must the autoflight servos be cleaned and greased?
    a. Every 500 flight hours or three years
    b. Every 1,000 flight hours or one year
    c. Every 1,000 flight hours or three years
    d. Every 500 flight hours or one year

29. When flying in U.S. airspace, what mode of transponder must be tested in accordance with FAR 91.411 and 91.413, Appendix F to ensure accurate altitude reporting?
    a. Mode A
    b. Mode X
    c. Mode S
    d. Mode F

30. Which of the following does NOT interface with the Boeing 747-400 Inertial Reference System (IRS)?
    a. Flight Management System (FMS)
    b. Central Maintenance Computer System (CMCS)
    c. Integrated Display System (IDS)
    d. Attitude Heading Reference System (AHRS)

31. Which of the following are all functions of the Boeing 747-400 Flight Management System (FMS)?
    a. Automatic radio tuning, lateral and vertical navigation, thrust management, and the display of flight plan maps
    b. Lateral and vertical navigation, thrust management, gear deployment, and flap position
    c. Thrust management, vertical and lateral navigation, and communications with flight service for flight plan updates
    d. Automatic radio tuning, lateral and vertical navigation, thrust management, the display of systems fault data

32. On the Boeing 747-400, the flight management system can be accessed from how many different Control Display Units (CDU)?
    a. One
    b. Two
    c. Three
    d. Four

33. What LRU on the B-747-400 flight management system is used to input preprogrammed navigational parameters, such as flight routes, waypoints, and airport data.
    a. The data loader
    b. The control display unit
    c. The EICAS control panel
    d. The mode select panel

34. On the B-747-400, what is the purpose of the autothrottle trimming system?
    a. A fine thrust adjustment to equalize the thrust of all four engines.
    b. A course throttle adjustment activated by the Fuel Control Units (FCU)
    c. A course throttle adjustment activated from the flight management computer.
    d. A fine throttle adjustment made by the EFIS/EICAS interface units (EIUs).

35. What is the only warning message displayed by the Boeing 747-400 EICAS related to the aircraft's flight management/autoflight system?
    a. A/P DISCONNECT
    b. FCC FAILURE
    c. IRU FAILURE
    d. YAW DAMPER INOP

36. The yaw damper system is designed to prevent which undesirable flight characteristic?
    a. Yaw roll
    b. Structural modal oscillations
    c. Lateral yaw
    d. Lateral modal oscillations

Chapter 6: Autopilot and Autoflight Systems

ANALYSIS QUESTIONS

name:

date:

1. A flight director is often integrated into the operation of the aircraft's autoflight systems. The flight director receives a variety of information from the autoflight system to drive the Attitude Director Indicator (ADI). Describe the six indications on the following ADI diagram.

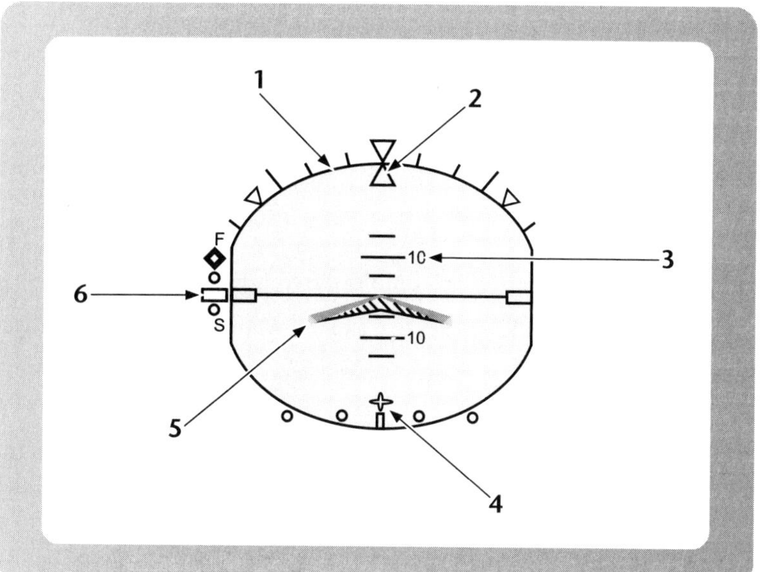

1. ______________________
2. ______________________
3. ______________________
4. ______________________
5. ______________________
6. ______________________

2. Accelerometers are a vital part of any autopilot system. Use textbook Figures 6-3-6 and 6-3-7 and the related readings to answer the following questions concerning accelerometers.

   a. On most aircraft, how many accelerometers are used to monitor each axis? ______________________

   b. Name the three axes that are typically monitored by accelerometers for autoflight systems. ______________________

   c. What is the accelerometer subsystem used to keep the accelerometer armature centered over the pick-off coils? ______________________

   d. Since acceleration is made up of magnitude and direction, it is considered what type of force? ______________________

name:

date:

3. Modern aircraft monitor a variety of information concerning the air surrounding the aircraft. This information is known as air data. What type of air data system is described by the following?

   a. Which system incorporates both electrical and pneumatic instruments? ______

   b. This system relies solely on static and pitot pressures to drive the air data instruments. ______

4. Flux detectors are commonly found on complex aircraft to provide compass data to the autoflight systems. Use textbook Figures 6-5-1 to 6-5-4 and the related readings to answer the following questions.

   a. What is another common term used to describe flux detectors? ______

   b. Where are flux detectors typically located on the aircraft? ______

   c. What is the voltage and frequency of the excitation voltage used by flux detectors? ______

   d. What systems monitor the output signals from a flux detector? Name all that apply. ______

5. Synchro feedback systems are transformer-like devices used to monitor the movement of control surfaces. Use your knowledge of synchro systems to answer the following questions.

   a. Synchro systems typically operate using what type of voltage? Be specific. ______

   b. If a synchro is in the null position what is the output voltage? Be specific. ______

   c. As the synchro rotor moves through the null position, what effect does this have on the phase of the output signal? ______

   d. Where are the most accurate synchro measurements obtained? ______

Chapter 6: Autopilot and Autoflight Systems

ANALYSIS QUESTIONS

name:

date:

6. Electric servos are often used to move the control surfaces according to autopilot commands. Electric servo mechanisms typically have common input and output signals required for operation. Label the five input/output signals needed for servo operation on the lines below.

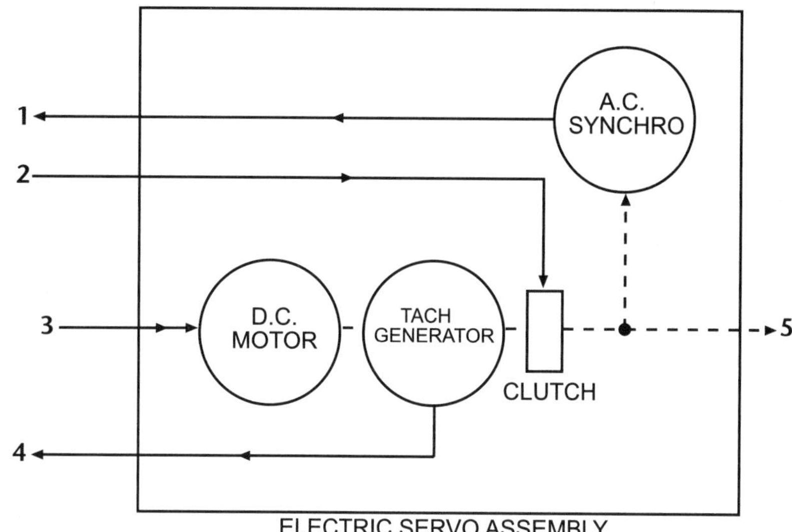

1. ______________________________

2. ______________________________

3. ______________________________

4. ______________________________

5. ______________________________

7. A typical corporate aircraft would contain one or more control panels for the autopilot system. Define the following controls of the autopilot controls found in Figures 6-8-2 and 6-8-3 in the textbook.

    a. What is the function of the engage/disengage switch? ______________________________

    b. What is the function of the ALT push button? ______________________________

    c. What is the function of the NAV mode? ______________________________

    d. What is the function of the AP XFR push button? ______________________________

ANALYSIS QUESTIONS

name:

date:

8. The Collins APS–85 is a very popular autopilot found on a variety of light jet and turboprop aircraft. Use your knowledge of data bus systems, electrical schematics and textbook Figure 6-8-4 to answer the following questions.

   a. Which autopilot channel can transmit data to the EFIS? ______

   b. What type of data is transmitted from the air data systems to the FCCs? Provide a specific data bus format. ______

   c. What voltage is used to engage the servo clutch mechanisms? Provide value and units. ______

   d. List the three ways the autopilot can be disengaged.

      1. ______

      2. ______

      3. ______

9. Answer the following questions according to the Collins APS-85 autopilot system shown in textbook Figure 6-8-4 and described in the related readings.

   a. Which LRU(s) is/are capable of sending ARINC 429 data to the FCC? Name all that apply. ______

   b. What types of signals are sent from the APP to the FCC for pitch and roll commands? ______

   c. Yaw damper signals are sent to which channel(s) of the FCC? ______

10. List the four major functions of the Phenom Flight Guidance and Control System (FGCS)

Chapter 6: Autopilot and Autoflight Systems

ANALYSIS QUESTIONS

name:

date:

11. The Boeing 747-400 Flight Management System (FMS) is an elaborate autoflight system typical of those found on transport category aircraft. The FMS sends and/or receives data to/from a variety of LRUs. Use textbook Figures 6-9-8 through 6-9-11 and related readings to answer the following questions.

    a. What unit is used by pilots to enter data for the FMS? ____________________

    b. What system is used to feed data from the FMC to the Central Maintenance Computer System (CMCS)? ____________________

    c. Which thrust levers contain the autothrottle disconnect switches? ____________________

    d. How many flight management computers are used in the B-747-400 FMS? __________

12. The Boeing 747-400 autothrottle system is part of the Flight Management System used to set engine thrust. Use Figures 6-9-11 through 6-9-13 in the textbook and related readings to answer the following questions concerning the autothrottle system.

    a. The Mode Control Panel (MCP) sends autothrottle command signals to which two units?

    b. Which LRU controls coarse adjustment of engine thrust? ____________________

    c. Which unit controls the fine adjustment of engine thrust? ____________________

    d. What voltage is sent from the left/right FMCs to control the autothrottle servos? Be specific and provide voltage value(s) and unit(s) for excitation and forward/reverse signals.

    e. The autothrottle servomotor generator transmits two output signals, tach feedback high and tach feedback low. These signals are set to which LRU? ____________________

Chapter 6: Autopilot and Autoflight Systems

ANALYSIS QUESTIONS

name:

date:

13. The Boeing 747-400 Autopilot Flight Director System receives input commands from the Mode Control Panel (MCP). Identify the eight controls on the following MCP diagram.

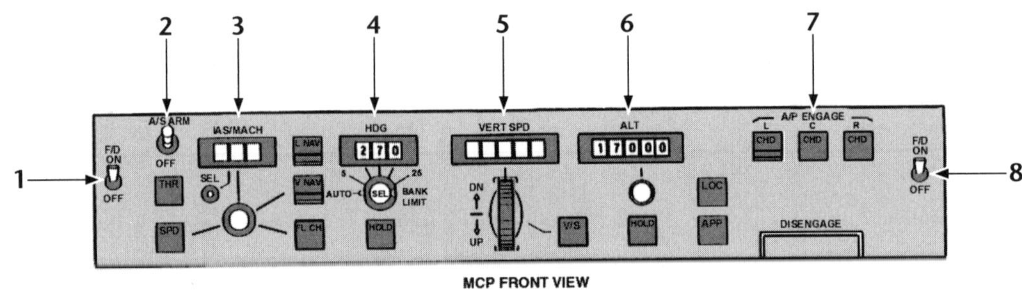

MCP FRONT VIEW

1. ____________________
2. ____________________
3. ____________________
4. ____________________
5. ____________________
6. ____________________
7. ____________________
8. ____________________

14. List the three distinct segments of the B-777 automatic flight control system.

1. ____________________
2. ____________________
3. ____________________

15. The B-747-400 Flight Control Computer receives input signals from a variety of systems. Use Figures 6-9-18 and 6-9-19 in the textbook, and related readings to answer the following questions.

a. Name the triple redundant sensors that send data to the FMC. ____________________

b. Warning data from the FCCs is transmitted through which LRU to the captain's and first officer's master warning lights? Provide full name and acronym. ____________________

Chapter 6: Autopilot and Autoflight Systems

ANALYSIS QUESTIONS

name:

date:

16. Textbook Figure 6-9-20 shows the interface connections for the B-747-400 Flight Control Computers. According to this figure what are the power inputs to the left FCC for the following? Provide voltage value, voltage units and the bus name supplying the power.

    a. Power inputs for warning annunciator ______________________________

    b. Power inputs for the FCC ______________________________

    c. Servo power ______________________________

17. The yaw damper system is used to control modal oscillations on transport category aircraft. Use textbook Figure 6-9-22 and related readings to answer the following questions concerning the Boeing 747-400 yaw damper system.

    a. How many yaw damper actuators are installed in the system? ______________________________

    b. What unit sends power to the yaw damper modules? ______________________________

    c. Where is the upper yaw damper actuator located? Be specific. ______________________________

18. What are the two major categories (systems) of flight controls on the B-777?

Chapter 6:

Autopilot and Autoflight Systems

ANALYSIS QUESTIONS

name:

date:

19. Name the three numbered LRUs shown in the B-777 automatic flight control system block diagram below.

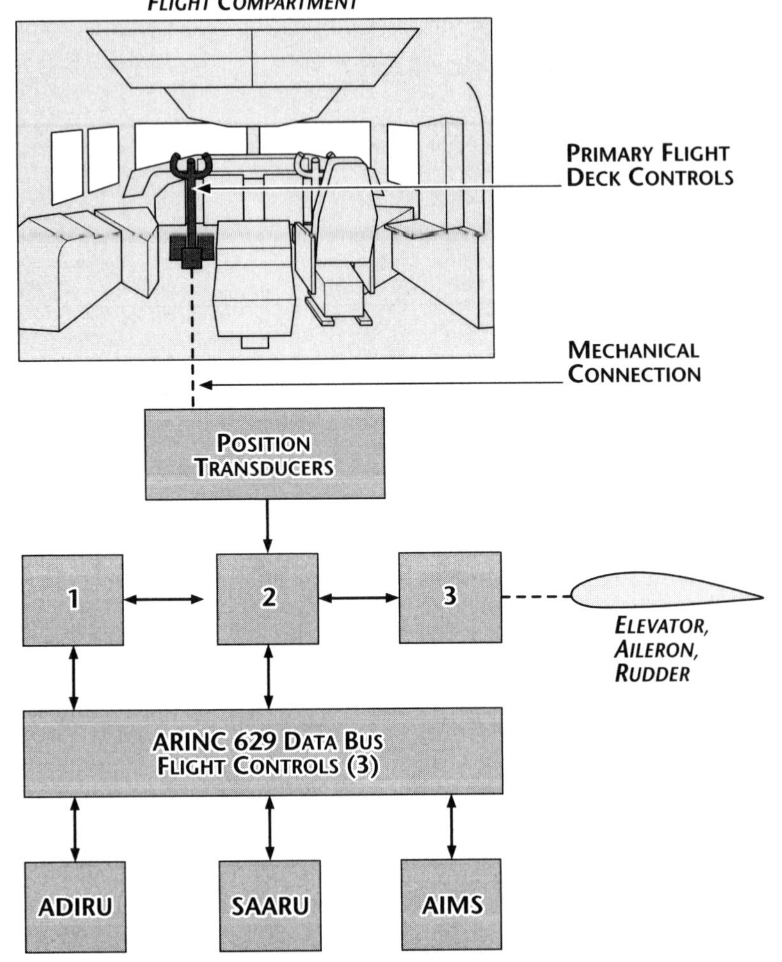

1. ______________________________

2. ______________________________

3. ______________________________

20. List the three types of servo actuators used on the A-380.

1. ______________________________

2. ______________________________

3. ______________________________

Chapter 7: Communication and Entertainment Systems

FILL IN THE BLANK QUESTIONS

name:

date:

1. ______________________________ is a digital air/ground communications service designed to reduce the amount of voice communications on the increasingly crowded VHF frequencies that allows ground-to-aircraft communications (in a digital format) for operational flight information, such as fuel status, flight delays, gate changes, departure times, and arrival times.

2. ______________ is the name of the ACARS service provided by ARINC Incorporated.

3. Virtually all transport category aircraft transmit OOOI data using ACARS. The OOOI stands for __________, __________, __________, and __________.

4. The ACARS system is designed to use a variety of VHF frequencies from __________ MHz to __________ MHz. In North America all ACARS transmissions begin on __________ MHz.

5. On the B-747-400, there is typically only one ACARS MU that is located in the main equipment center. The two power sources required by the ACARS MU are 115 VAC from ______________, and 28 VDC from the ______________ bus.

6. The ACARS control is managed through any one of the three ______________.

7. On the B-747-400, the ______________ is used for radio selection and tuning for the HF and VHF radios.

8. The ______________ is found on transport category aircraft to provide communications between flight crew, ground crew, flight attendants and maintenance personnel.

9. The four basic subsystems of B-747-400 interphone system are the __________ interphone, the __________ interphone, the __________ interphone and the __________ system.

10. The B-747-400 ______________ system is used to provide communications between flight crewmembers and/or other aircraft operations personnel.

11. The ______________ is located in the main equipment bay and is used to process and control all audio signals required by the flight crew.

12. The ______________ provide command signals to the B-747-400 AMU for control of the communication and navigation audio signals.

13. The ______________ system permits ground crew communications through various access points located throughout the B-747-400 aircraft. Technicians often use this portion of the interphone system during various maintenance operations and also during ground service operations.

Chapter 7: Communication and Entertainment Systems

FILL IN THE BLANK QUESTIONS

name:

date:

14. The ____________________ is used to alert ground crew personnel of an interphone message from the flight crew, and to alert the flight crew of a message from the ground crew.

15. The ____________________ receives input signals from the service interphone jacks and coordinates interphone system communications.

16. Systems that allow laptops, WiFi enabled personal digital assistants (PDA) and other wireless devices to connect to the World Wide Web during flight are called ____________________.

17. The ____________________ is used on the B-747-400 to control the passenger entertainment audio system, the cabin interphone system, cabin lighting, the passenger service system, and the passenger address system.

18. In order for the Aircell system to provide the air-to-ground link, the ACPU sends passenger data to the ____________________.

19. The ____________________/____________________ are used to interface ACESS with the central maintenance computer system and the integrated display units.

20. On the B-747-400 each ____________________ is comprised of three independent circuits, one dedicated to each main controller.

21. The ____________________ / ____________________ controls the Passenger Entertainment System (PES) audio to the passenger headphones, Cabin Lighting System (CLS), and the Passenger Service System (PSS).

22. The ____________________ controls the Passenger Address System (PAS) audio output to the cabin speakers and passenger headphones.

23. The ____________________ is a digital interface unit used to coordinate programming, testing and monitoring of ACESS and receives inputs from the cabin configuration test module, the software data loader, and the EFIS/EICAS interface units.

24. The software data loader is used to program ____________________ in the event of an aircraft configuration change.

25. The LACs act as a distribution unit for each of the three main controllers and send lighting commands and digitized audio signals to the ____________________ and the ____________________ for distribution to the individual passenger stations and lighting circuits.

26. The ACESS ____________________ control the overhead speakers, cabin lighting, passenger reading lights, flight attendant call lights, and passenger information lights (no smoking, and fasten seat belts).

Chapter 7: Communication and Entertainment Systems

FILL IN THE BLANK QUESTIONS

name:

date:

27. The B-747-400 PAS automatic volume adjustment system is used to set ______________________ volume levels according to the amount of cabin noise.

28. The ______________________ are used to interface with the each seat control for selecting various audio channels, volume, reading lights, and attendant call lights.

29. The ______________________ is the software program that is used to inform ACESS of the current cabin layout.

30. The ______________________ is the central multiplexer/demultiplexer for the CIS.

31. On the B-747-400 the ______________________ provides communications between different flight attendant stations and between flight attendant stations and the flight deck.

32. A ______________________ alert call can be made from any flight attendant station and overrides all other interphone operations except another pilot alert call.

33. The ______________________ transmits audio through a series of cabin speakers to announce messages from the flight crew, flight attendants, the prerecorded tape reproducer (messages and boarding music), the videotape reproducer (audio only), or to sound cabin chimes.

34. The ______________________ is one of the three main ACESS controllers, and provides the main coordinating functions for the PAS.

35. The ______________________ audio provides prerecorded audio signals to each passenger seat interface unit and typically contains several channels of music or other entertainment audio, as well as the audio portion of any in-flight movie (video) presentation.

36. The ______________________ / ______________________ is the main ACESS controller, which coordinates the distribution of the audiotape reproducer and the passenger video system audio signals.

37. The ______________________ is used to control reading lights and attendants call functions. It is also used to control passenger information signs and attendant call functions from the lavatory.

38. The ______________________ is part of ACESS that controls indirect ceiling lights, sidewall wash lights, direct ceiling lights, and night-lights.

39. The B-747-400 ACESS contains test circuitry to help diagnose system faults. The status check function can be performed during flight or on the ground to retrieve failure data stored in the ______________ memory.

Chapter 7: Communication and Entertainment Systems

FILL IN THE BLANK QUESTIONS

name:

date:

40. When requested by the technician, the ACESS CMU sends all fault data to ________________ that can be used to perform system status checks, system tests, and software configuration updates and verifications.

41. The ACESS ________________ feature allows technicians to run real-time tests of the various ACESS LRUs and can only be performed on the ground.

42. The ________________ function initiated through the CCTM is used to test the attendant master call lights, the row call lights, the lavatory call lights, and the passenger information sign lights.

43. The ________________ software is used to instruct ACESS LRUs how to function in the system, and is typically installed in the shop prior to the LRU reaching the aircraft.

44. The ________________ database is used by the LRUs to determine the specific layout of the aircraft's cabin and is typically installed into an LRU's memory after the LRU has been installed in the aircraft.

45. The ________________ is used to display video entertainment on various monitors and/or projectors located throughout the cabin. The system uses prerecorded VHS format tapes that contain both the video and audio tracks.

46. The ________________ is the major control and distribution unit for the entertainment video signals. It receives video and audio inputs from the Video Tape Reproducer (VTR) and a discrete signal from the decompression relay.

47. On the B-747-400 the VSCU is located under the stairway to the upper deck in the ________________.

48. The A-380 cabin communications and in flight entertainment systems are part of the A-380 ________________ .

Chapter 7:
Communication and Entertainment Systems

MULTIPLE CHOICE QUESTIONS

name:

date:

1. ACARS is typically found on which of the following type of aircraft?
   a. Light aircraft
   b. Corporate aircraft
   c. Transport category aircraft
   d. All aircraft assigned to an instrument flight plan

2. Which of the following statements best describes the type of data transmitted by the airborne equipment of ACARS?
   a. ACARS is used for transmission of analog communications signals to air traffic control.
   b. ACARS is used for transmission of digital weather information from the FAA flight service.
   c. ACARS is used for digital data transmission of operational flight information, such as fuel status, flight delays, and gate changes.
   d. ACARS is used for analog transmission of aircraft status data, such as engine vibrations and systems fault data.

3. What does the acronym ACARS stand for?
   a. Aircraft Coordination Application and Reporting System
   b. Airborne Communication Addressing and Reporting System
   c. Aircraft Compliance Achievement and Registration System
   d. ARINC Coordination Advancement and Reassignment System

4. While ACARS is operating in the demand mode, which of the following is true?
   a. The flight crew or airborne equipment initiates communications.
   b. The airline ground facilities initiate communications.
   c. The FAA en route controllers initiate communications with the aircraft ACARS.
   d. The ARINC headquarters initiate all communications with the airborne equipment.

5. The airborne ACARS transmissions are made through which of the following radios?
   a. A dedicated ACARS receiver/transmitter (R/T)
   b. A SATCOM R/T
   c. The aircraft's UHF communications R/T
   d. The aircraft's VHF communications transceiver

6. Which of the following is an international corporation that provides two-way satellite communication services in remote regions or where there is no reliable ground-based network?
   a. ARINC
   b. ICAO
   c. Aircell
   d. Inmarsat

7. Which of the following statements best describe the function of the flight interphone system found on transport category aircraft?
   a. The flight interphone system is used to provide communications between flight crewmembers and/or other aircraft operations personnel.
   b. The flight interphone system is used to provide communications between flight crewmembers and aircraft passengers
   c. The flight interphone system is used to provide communications between airline operations and the flight crew.
   d. The flight interphone system is used to provide communications between ground crewmembers during maintenance operations.

8. On the B-747-400, the LRU used by the pilots to control audio inputs/outputs for communication and navigation systems is the:
   a. Audio Control Panels (ACP)
   b. Control Display Units (CDU)
   c. Audio Management Unit (AMU)
   d. Radio Tuning Unit (RTU)

9. Generally speaking, on transport category aircraft what microphone(s) are available at the captain's station?
   a. A hand held microphone
   b. The oxygen mask microphone
   c. The captain's headset microphone
   d. All of the above

Chapter 7: Communication and Entertainment Systems

MULTIPLE CHOICE QUESTIONS

name:

date:

10. On the B-747-400, which of the following is a carbon-type microphone for the flight crew?
    a. The hand held microphone
    b. The oxygen mask microphone
    c. The captain's headset microphone
    d. Due to poor quality, carbon-type microphones are not used on transport category aircraft

11. On the B-747-400, how many different service interphone connection points are available for ground crew communications?
    a. 6
    b. 10
    c. 19
    d. 34

12. On the B-747-400, a horn assembly is located in the nose wheel well. The horn will sound to alert ground crew to which of the following?
    a. A flight deck interphone call is made to the ground crew, the engine throttles have been moved to the start position, or the aircraft flaps are in motion.
    b. The engine throttles have been moved to the start position, a flight deck interphone call is made to the ground crew, or there is an equipment cooling system failure.
    c. The flight crew is requesting a ground crew member to come to the flight deck, the aircraft is ready to taxi, or a flight deck interphone call is made to the ground crew.
    d. A flight deck interphone call is made to the ground crew, there is an equipment cooling system failure, or the inertial reference unit is on and AC power is not supplied to the aircraft.

13. Generally speaking, which of the following would be the most common component to fail in any crew communications system?
    a. The ARINC 429 data bus connections
    b. The microphones, headsets, and related connections
    c. The system LRUs
    d. The system multiplexers and demultiplexers

14. What is the minimum altitude where an aircraft can receive reliable Aircell broadband service?
    a. 1,000 ft.
    b. 4,000 ft.
    c. 6,000 ft.
    d. 10,000 ft.

15. The Advanced Cabin Entertainment Service System (ACESS) found on the B-747-400 is controlled the following system(s).
    a. The passenger entertainment audio system
    b. The cabin interphone system
    c. The cabin lighting
    d. All of the above

16. Which of the following statements best describes the audio signal transmission of the B-747-400 ACESS?
    a. All audio transmissions through ACESS are made in analog format.
    b. All audio transmissions are digital ARINC 429 format until they reach the seat electronics unit.
    c. ARINC 629 is used to distribute audio throughout the aircraft.
    d. ACESS employs multiplexers to change parallel data into a serial format for distribution throughout the aircraft.

17. Which of the following is NOT considered one of the main ACESS controllers?
    a. Passenger Address Controller (PAC)
    b. Cabin Interphone Controller (CIC)
    c. Entertainment/Service Controller (ESC)
    d. Local Area Controller (LAC)

Chapter 7: Communication and Entertainment Systems

MULTIPLE CHOICE QUESTIONS

name:

date:

18. Which B-747-400 ACESS LRU is used to perform system status checks, system tests, and software configuration updates?
    a. The Control Display Unit (CDU)
    b. The secondary EICAS display
    c. The EICAS maintenance page function
    d. The Cabin Configuration Test Module (CCTM)

19. On the Boeing 747-400, which of the following ACESS LRUs are used for distribution of lighting commands and digitized audio signals to the individual passenger stations?
    a. Entertainment/Service Controller (ESC)
    b. Overhead Electronic Units (OEU) and Seat Electronic Units (SEU)
    c. Control Management Unit (CMU)
    d. Cabin Interphone Controller (CIC)

20. Which ACESS LRU(s) are used to control the cabin speakers, cabin lighting, passenger reading lights, flight attendant call lights, and passenger information lights (no smoking, and fasten seat belts)?
    a. The Seat Electronics Units
    b. The Overhead Electronic Units
    c. The Passenger Address Controller
    d. The Cabin Configuration Test Module

21. Each cabin handset used for cabin interphone communications are connected to one of four ______________ which connect the handsets to the Cabin Interphone Controller.
    a. Local Area Controllers (LAC)
    b. Overhead electronics units (OEU)
    c. MAWEA
    d. Passenger Address Controller (PAC)

22. The Cabin Systems Modules (CSM) are used by the flight attendants to control cabin lighting. CSM commands are sent to the ESC where they are distributed to the appropriate LACs. Which of the following statements best describe how the LACs then control the lights?
    a. The LAC sends a signal to the appropriate Overhead Electronics Unit (OEU). The OEU then turns on the appropriate cabin lights.
    b. The LAC turns on the lights directly.
    c. The LAC sends a command signal to the Seat Electronics Units (SEU) that turns on the appropriate cabin lights.
    d. The LAC directly controls fluorescent lighting. All other lights are controlled through the overhead electronics units.

23. The cabin interphone system has a priority program that routes calls according to their importance. Which of the following has the highest call priority?
    a. All call
    b. Attendants' all call
    c. Priority line calls
    d. Pilot alert call

24. Which main ACESS controller is used for the cabin chime system?
    a. Passenger Address Controller (PAC)
    b. Cabin Interphone Controller (CIC)
    c. Entertainment/Service Controller (ESC)
    d. Local Area Controller (LAC)

25. The Passenger Address Controller (PAC) software contains an automatic volume adjustment circuitry to increase PA volume as cabin noise increases. Under which of the following conditions will the PA volume increase the most?
    a. Decompression
    b. Take off
    c. Tax
    d. Cruise

Chapter 7: Communication and Entertainment Systems

MULTIPLE CHOICE QUESTIONS

name:

date:

26. Which of the following statements best describes the Passenger Entertainment System (PES) portion of ACESS?
    a. The PES controls all video and audio signals in a digital multiplexed format.
    b. The PES is a multi-channel digital audio system that transmits audio directly to the passengers' headsets bypassing the OEUs and SEUs.
    c. The Digital Passenger Control Units (DPCU) demultiplexes all PES audio.
    d. The PES provides audio signals to each passenger SEU where the digital signal is converted to an analog signal and sent to the passengers' headphones.

27. On the B-747-400, one Local Area Controller (LAC) typically connects to a series of Seat Electronic Units (SEU) via a digital data bus. What must be installed at the end of the data bus to ensure proper data bus impedance?
    a. A 75-ohm termination plug
    b. A ground connector for the data bus shielding
    c. The data bus must return to the LAC
    d. The data bus must end at the last SEU in the series

28. Which subsystem of ACESS is used to control the passenger information signs no smoking, fasten seatbelts, and lavatory occupied?
    a. Passenger Service System (PSS)
    b. Entertainment/Service Controller (ESC)
    c. Passenger Entertainment System (PES)
    d. Cabin Interphone Controller (CIC)

29. On the B-747-400, where are the ACESS seat electronics units (SEU) typically located?
    a. SEUs are found in the electrical equipment bay near the ACESS controller.
    b. SEUs are behind plastic overhead panels in the passenger compartment.
    c. SEUs are mounted in the armrest of each seat.
    d. SEUs are mounted to the frame assembly of passenger seats.

30. On the B-747-400, which of the following EICAS messages may be displayed in the event of an ACESS system failure?
    a. An EICAS warning message
    b. An EICAS caution message
    c. An EICAS status message
    d. There are no ACESS messages displayed on EICAS

31. How many Local Area Controllers (LAC) are used in the B-747-400 Advanced Cabin Entertainment Service System?
    a. 1
    b. 2
    c. 3
    d. 4

32. Which of the following statements best describes the Boeing 747-400 ACESS configuration database software?
    a. The software must be modified if the cabin configuration is changed.
    b. Configuration software is typically installed into an LRU's memory after the LRU has been installed in the aircraft.
    c. The CCTM is used to down load configuration software from the Central Management Unit (CMU) to other ACESS LRUs.
    d. All of the above

Chapter 7: Communication and Entertainment Systems

ANALYSIS QUESTIONS

name:

date:

1. The Airborne Communications Addressing and Reporting System (ACARS) is a digital communications service for transmission of flight information, such as fuel status, flight delays, gate changes, departure times, and arrival times. Answer the following questions about ACARS according to textbook Figures 7-2-1 through 7-2-3 and related readings.

   a. Most ACARS transmit OOOI data to the airline operations center. What does OOOI stand for? __________

   b. On the Boeing 747-400, which LRU is used to load ACARS MU software? __________

   c. Where would the ACARS control display unit typically be located? __________

   d. Is there a one-way or two-way communications link between the ACARS Management Unit and the Flight Management Computers? __________

2. List the three levels of Inmarsat satellite communication services currently available for airborne use.

3. Answer the following questions according to the Boeing 747-400 flight interphone interface diagram in textbook Figure 7-3-1.

   a. List three components the captain can use to input audio signals to the MU. __________

   b. List the three components through which the captain can receive audio from the audio MU. __________

4. The B-747-400 flight interphone system is used to provide communications between flight crewmembers and/or other aircraft operations personnel. All flight interphone audio is controlled through the Audio Management Unit. Reference textbook Figures 7-3-3 and 7-3-4 to answer the following questions concerning the architecture of the flight interphone system.

   a. How many circuit breakers are used to power the Audio Management Unit? __________

   b. How many redundant circuit cards are contained in the AMU? __________

   c. If the captain's card experiences a short to ground, will the first officer's and first observer's cards operate normally, yes or no? Explain your answer. __________

   d. How many audio speakers are used in the system? __________

Chapter 7: Communication and Entertainment Systems

ANALYSIS QUESTIONS

name:

date:

5. The Service Interphone System is used by ground handling and maintenance personnel for ground communications. Answer the following questions according to the Boeing 747-400 service interphone locations diagram in textbook Figure 7-3-9.

   a. How many external sources are available for the service interphone connections? ______

   b. What external service interphone location is the farthest forward and at what station is it located? ______

   c. At what station number is the farthest aft internal service interphone connection? ______

6. List the numbered LRUs in the Aircell airborne component block diagram below.

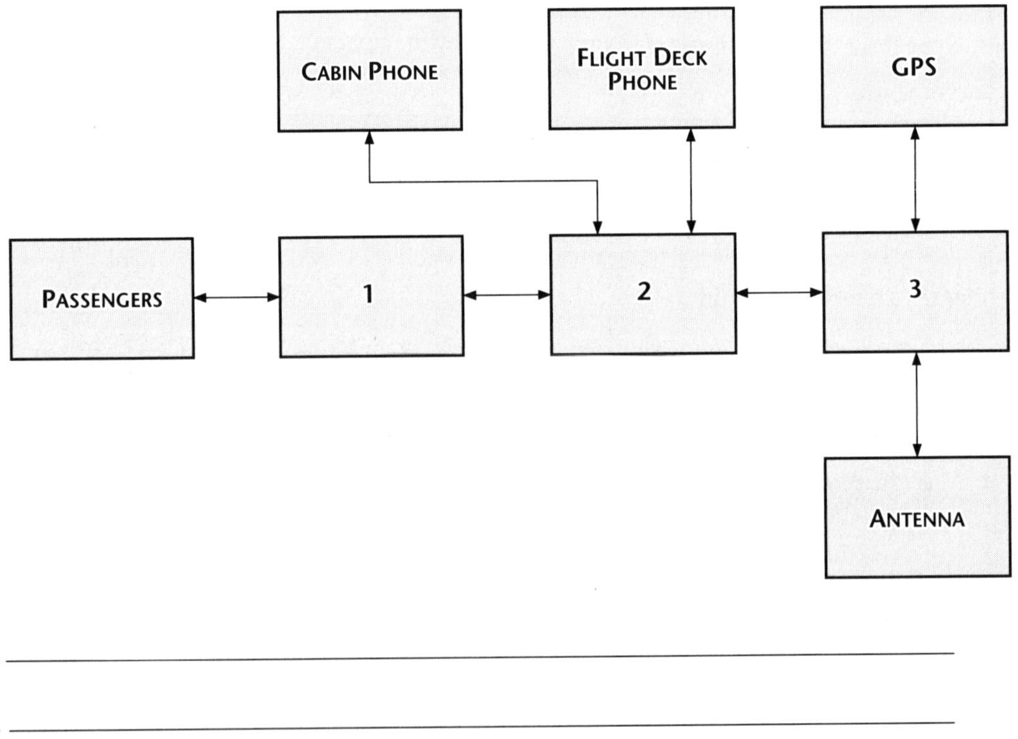

1. ______
2. ______
3. ______

7. List the four primary in-aircraft components used in the Aircell Broadband system.

Chapter 7:
Communication and Entertainment Systems

ANALYSIS QUESTIONS

name:

date:

8. The B-747-400 Advanced Cabin Entertainment Service System (ACESS) is used to control a variety of functions for passenger convenience systems and cabin lighting. Answer the following questions about ACESS according to textbook Figures 7-5-1 through 7-5-3 and the related readings.

    a. What are the five major subsystems of ACESS? ______________________________

    ____

    ____.

    b. What type of data format is used to transmit the majority of ACESS data: digital / analog and parallel / serial. ______________________________.

    c. What type of circuit is used to change serial digital data into parallel digital data? ________

    ____.

    d. What is the maximum number of seat electronics units that can be connected to one local area controller? ______________________________.

9. The major LRUs of the B-747-400 ACESS are shown in the following diagram. Use the table to record the names of each numbered LRU. Provide full LRU name and acronym.

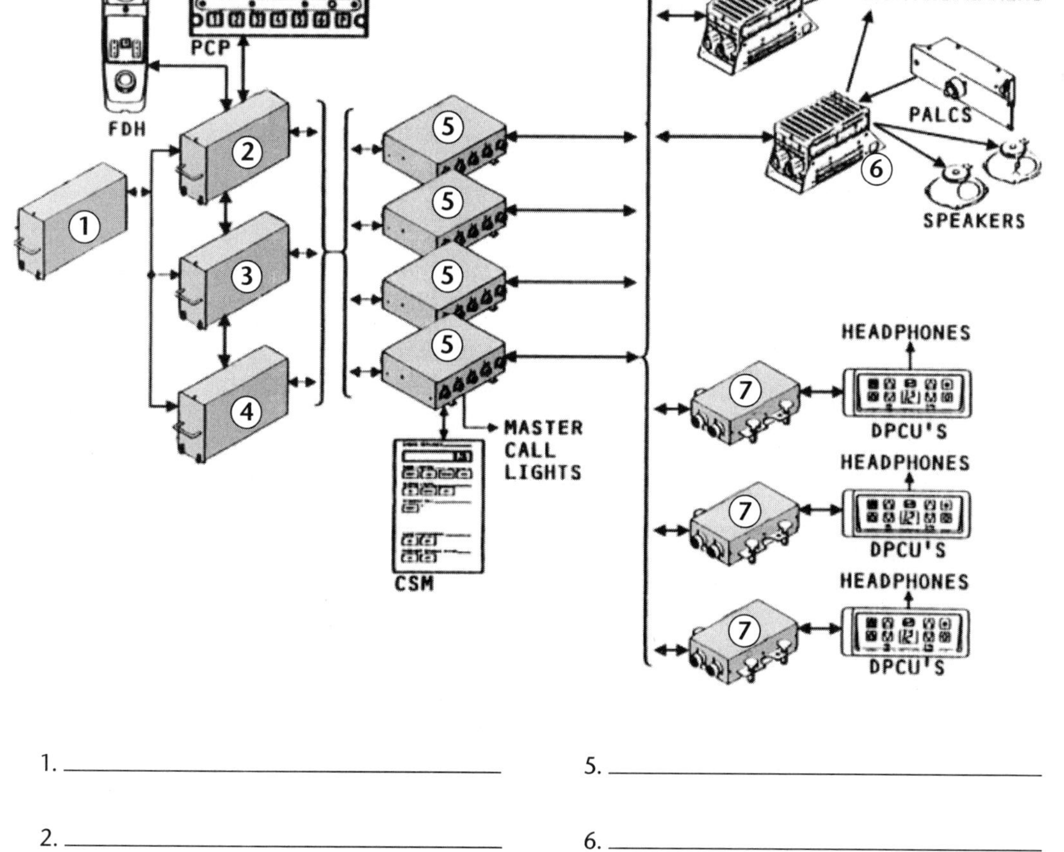

1. ______________________________ 5. ______________________________

2. ______________________________ 6. ______________________________

3. ______________________________ 7. ______________________________

4. ______________________________

Chapter 7:

Communication and Entertainment Systems

ANALYSIS QUESTIONS

name:

date:

10. According to the Boeing 747-400 ACESS pictorial diagram in Figure 7-5-5, what three controllers receive data from the ACESS central management unit? Provide full LRU name and the acronym.

11. The Passenger Address System (PAS) on the B-747-400 transmits audio through a series of cabin speakers to announce messages from: the flight crew, flight attendants, the prerecorded tape reproducer (messages and boarding music), the video tape reproducer (audio only), or to sound cabin chimes. Use your knowledge of the PAS, and Figure 7-5-10 and Table 7-5-2 in the textbook to answer the following questions.

    a. A prerecorded announcement is routed through three LRUs to reach a cabin speaker. Name the three LRUs. Provide both the LRU full name and the acronym. ____________

    b. Describe the format and type of signal used to send video system audio to the PAC. ____________

    c. What type of electrical signal is used to alert the PAC that the aircraft is airborne? ____________

    d. Which local area controller is used to send audio signals to the upper deck of the aircraft? ____________

12. The Passenger Address Controller (PAC) on the B-747-400 contains an automatic volume adjustment circuit for all passenger address audio. Use Figure 7-5-15 in the textbook to answer the following questions concerning the PAC.

    a. Which relay is used to identify that the oxygen lines are pressurized due to aircraft decompression? Provide relay name, relay number and panel number. ____________

    b. During cabin decompression what is the volume increase? ____________

    c. With the aircraft on the ground and engines off, what is the volume setting? ____________

    d. Under what flight configuration is the volume the greatest? ____________

Chapter 7: Communication and Entertainment Systems

ANALYSIS QUESTIONS

name:

date:

13. The passenger entertainment audio signals are multiplexed through a variety of LRUs. Use Figure 7-5-16 and Table 7-5-3 in the textbook to answer the following questions concerning passenger entertainment audio. Provide full LRU names for answers where applicable.

    a. Which unit multiplexes audio signals from the entertainment tape reproducer for distribution to the various SEUs? ______

    b. How many local area controllers are connected to the entertainment service controller? ______

    c. What is the function of the CCTM? ______

14. The passenger entertainment audio system is covered in textbook Figures 7-5-16 through 7-5-20. Uses these diagrams and related reading to answer the following questions.

    a. The last seat electronics unit is connected to the seat track ground through what component? ______

    b. What LRU is used by the passengers to input volume requests? ______

    c. How many audio channels are transmitted from the entertainment tape reproducer to the audio entertainment multiplexer? ______

    d. What is the maximum number of DPCUs that can interface with a seat electronics unit? ______

Chapter 7: Communication and Entertainment Systems

ANALYSIS QUESTIONS

name:

date:

15. The major LRUs of the B-747-400 Passenger Service System are shown in the following diagram. Record the names of each numbered LRU below. Include LRU complete name and acronym.

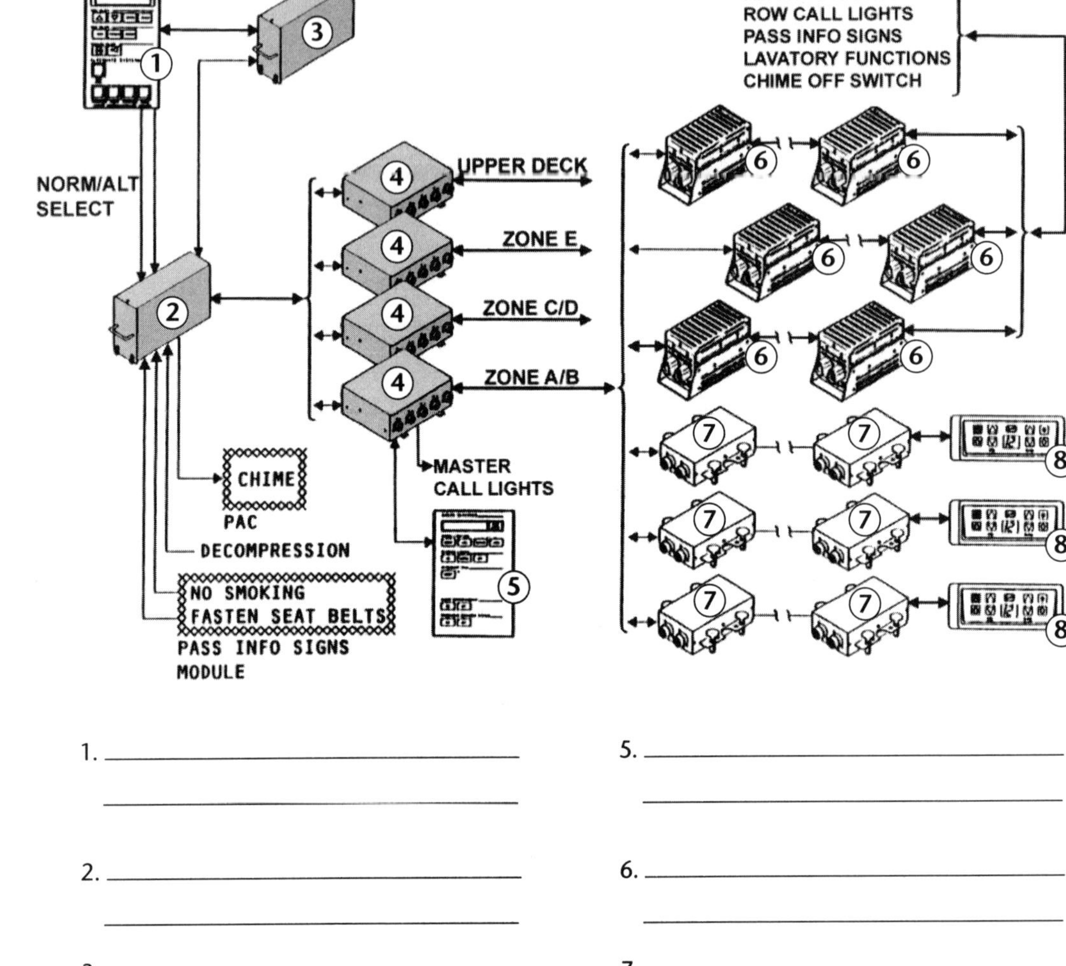

1. ______________________________
____

2. ______________________________
____

3. ______________________________
____

4. ______________________________
____

5. ______________________________
____

6. ______________________________
____

7. ______________________________
____

8. ______________________________
____

16. Describe the difference between the ACESS system status check and the ACESS system tests as they apply to the Boeing 747-400.

Chapter 7:
Communication and Entertainment Systems

ANALYSIS QUESTIONS

name:

date:

17. During troubleshooting, ACESS fault data is displayed on the Cabin Configuration Test Module (CCTM). Describe the information presented in the following CCTM display.

CCTM DISPLAY — 1
FAILURE 002 OF 004 — 2
PROGRAM LINE ERROR — 3
LAC 1 DOOR 2 LEFT FWD — 4
OEU 1-2- ROW 5 — 5

1. ______________________
2. ______________________
3. ______________________
4. ______________________
5. ______________________

18. The Boeing 747-400 passenger entertainment system video is distributed to various monitors and projection units located throughout the aircraft. Name the LRUs presented in the following PES video diagram. Provide the full LRU name and acronym, if applicable.

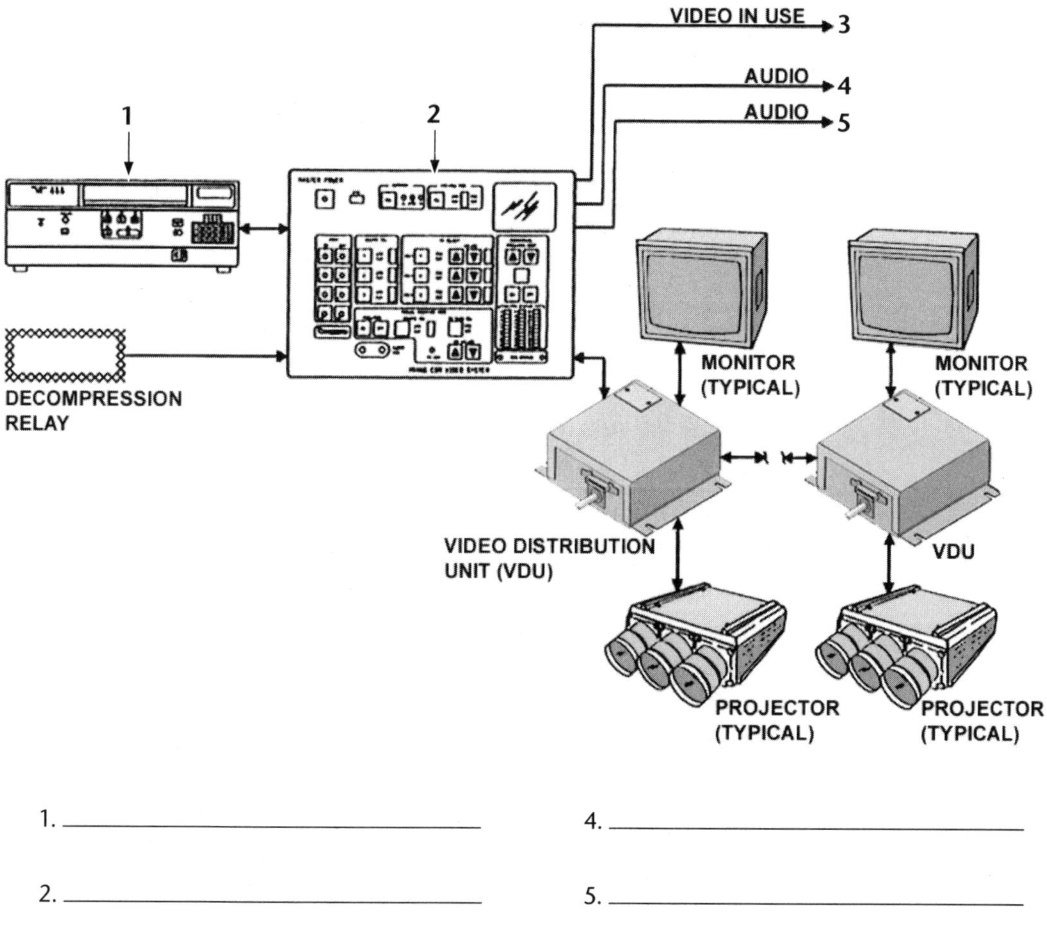

1. ______________________
2. ______________________
3. ______________________
4. ______________________
5. ______________________

Chapter 7: Communication and Entertainment Systems

ANALYSIS QUESTIONS

name:

date:

19. List the five main LRUs needed for operation of the B-777 passenger entertainment system. List the acronym and the full name.

Chapter 8: Global Positioning System

FILL IN THE BLANK QUESTIONS

name:

date:

1. The ______________________________ is a satellite-based system that is capable of providing position and navigational data for ground based and airborne receivers.

2. The navigational capabilities of GPS are determined through multiple calculations and comparison to the ______________________________ map.

3. In the United States, the formal name for the global positioning system is the ________________ GPS.

4. The NAVSTAR GPS consists of three distinct elements: the ____________________ segment, the ____________________ segment, and the ____________________ segment.

5. The GPS satellites are each placed in a near geosynchronous orbit approximately ______________ nm (______________ km) (insert number) above the earth and are equally spaced around six different orbits to provide worldwide coverage.

6. Each satellite in the system transmits position and precise time information on two frequencies known as L_1 that operates at ______________ MHz and L_2 that operates at ______________ MHz. (insert numbers)

7. The individual satellites are identified by the information broadcasted by the modulated carrier waves, which is achieved through a process known as ____________________________ .

8. The control segment of the GPS system consists of ______________ ground-based monitor stations, ______________ master control station, and ______________ (insert numbers) ground antennas located at different sites throughout the world.

9. The GPS user segment is typically designed to receive time and position data from ______________ (insert number) or more satellites and process that data into the desired output.

10. Using time and velocity to derive distance (range) is known as the ______________________ ranging concept.

11. In most cases, the GPS receiver/processor incorporates a low-cost ______________________ crystal controlled oscillator, which will establish a given frequency.

12. The four most common GPS errors are ____________________ errors, ____________________ errors, ____________________ errors, and ____________________ errors.

13. The digital codes transmitted by the GPS satellites are known as the ________________/ ________________ (C/A) code and the ________________ (P) code, which contain the timing and satellite position information required by the receiver to calculate navigational data.

Chapter 8: Global Positioning System

FILL IN THE BLANK QUESTIONS

name:

date:

14. The four limitations of using GPS for civilian aircraft are defined as ________________, ________________, ________________, and ________________.

15. ________________ was designed to increase the accuracy, availability, integrity and continuity of the basic GPS to a level sufficient for complete aircraft navigation.

16. Most experts agree that in the future differential GPS will become a primary navigation source for both ________________ and ________________ landings worldwide.

17. In 1993 the FAA approved a non-precision GPS approach, commonly called the ________________.

18. The TSO ensures a minimum quality and accuracy standard set by the ____________.

19. The ________________ is a type of differential GPS designed for use during Category II or Category III precision approach.

20. As of 1996, all equipment certified under TSO-____________ (insert number/letters) allowed pilots to utilize the GPS as supplemental area navigation equipment.

21. Two of the most common airborne GPS features are the extended ________________ and the ________________ map display.

22. The airborne GPS equipment may contain an option called the ________________ display to provide a real time horizontal "picture" of the aircraft and surrounding navigational reference points.

23. A GPS moving map display provides a horizontal "picture" of the aircraft and surrounding ________________ reference points.

24. Many airborne GPS receivers are combined into one unit with a conventional ____________ transceiver.

25. In the GPS receiver, the ________________ is used to filter out any extraneous signals and convert the RF input from the antenna to a given intermediate frequency (IF).

26. The quartz clock/frequency synthesizer provides the master ____________ pulse and is the source of all reference frequencies within the receiver/processor.

27. All GPS airborne receivers must be able to acquire and track the satellite range code information, determine the ________________ (PR) from each satellite, and demodulate the 50Hz navigation message.

28. The data processor uses the calculated range measurements and a ____________ Hz (insert number) NAV message to solve for position, velocity, and time (PVT).

Chapter 8: Global Positioning System

FILL IN THE BLANK QUESTIONS

name:

date:

29. The data processors perform their calculations using an advance software algorithm known as the ____________________ filter.

30. The KLN90 can present position and course deviation information on its own LCD display or the unit can interface with a CDI, EFIS or ______________________________ .

31. The Bendix/King KLN-90B can be installed for __________ or __________ certification.

32. For all airborne GPS equipment, it is important that the antenna be mounted in a location so it is level ± _______________ degrees (insert number) when the aircraft is in level flight to ensure that satellites close to the horizon are captured.

33. To ensure communication signals do not interfere with satellite reception, the airborne GPS antenna must be mounted at least _______________ feet (insert number) from any communications antenna.

34. Antenna coaxial cable for airborne GPS equipment has a maximum allowable loss of _______________ dB (insert number) and is critical for proper airborne GPS operation.

35. When connecting the GPS KLN90 receiver/processor to various aircraft systems ____________________ may be used to configure the GPS to the particular installation.

36. Two common sources of interference for airborne GPS receivers are the communication (COM) radio and the ______________________________ .

Chapter 8: Global Positioning System

MULTIPLE CHOICE QUESTIONS

name:

date:

1. What is the formal name for the United States global positioning system that was assigned by the Department of Defense in 1973?
   a. Glanoss
   b. NAVSTAR GPS
   c. World Geodetic System
   d. SpaceNav GPS

2. In the United States system, what is the total number of satellites in the GPS space segment? How many satellites are in active use and how many are spares?
   a. There are 16 orbiting satellites; 15 of the satellites are active and one spare.
   b. There are 13 orbiting satellites; 10 of the satellites are active and three are spares.
   c. There are 41 orbiting satellites; 34 of the satellites are active and seven are spares.
   d. There are 24 orbiting satellites; 21 of the satellites are active and three are spares.

3. What are the operating frequencies of L_1 and L_2 that are used for the transmission of position and precise time information by GPS satellites?
   a. L_1 operates at 1,575.42 KHz and L_2 operates at 1,227.6 KHz.
   b. L_1 operates at 1,575.42 MHz and L_2 operates at 1,227.6 MHz.
   c. L_1 operates at 650.64 MHz and L_2 operates at 720.33 MHz.
   d. L_1 operates at 650.64 KHz and L_2 operates at 720.33 KHz.

4. The GPS receiver/processor initially calculates range, which includes a time bias error. This range (containing the time base error) is known as:
   a. Pseudorange
   b. Time based range
   c. Delta range
   d. Time of arrival

5. Extremely accurate timing signals are required for the operation of GPS. How do the space and user segments of GPS ensure correct timing?
   a. The satellites and receiver/processors contain an atomic clock.
   b. The satellites and receiver/processors contain a temperature compensated free running oscillator.
   c. The satellites contain an atomic clock and send accurate timing data to the receiver/processors.
   d. The ground-based control segment of GPS monitors an atomic clock and sends accurate timing data to each satellite and the satellites send timing signals to each receiver/processor.

6. There are several types of errors that can affect the accuracy of GPS data. What is the cause of Ephemeris errors?
   a. Ephemeris errors are caused by the distortion of the transmitted signal.
   b. Ephemeris errors are caused by variations in the satellite clock system.
   c. Ephemeris errors are caused by slight variations in the satellites orbit.
   d. Ephemeris errors are caused by local electrical noise (interference).

7. What general equation is used to calculate actual range from a series of GPS satellites?
   a. Actual range (R) equals pseudorange (PR) less the satellite clock errors (SCE).
   b. Actual range (R) equals pseudorange (PR) less the receiver error (RE).
   c. Actual range (R) equals pseudorange (PR) less the atmospheric propagation error (APE).
   d. Actual range (R) equals pseudorange (PR) less the range error (E).

8. Which of the following statements is true concerning the GPS course/acquisition (C/A) code and the precision (P) code?
   a. The C/A-and P-code data transmits a total of 25 different data frames at 50bits/second and contains 1,500bits/frame.
   b. The C/A-code data is broadcast on VHF frequencies and the P-code data is broadcast on UHF frequencies.
   c. The C/A-code is a digital clock signal and the P-code is an analog satellite identification signal.
   d. In order to ensure full reception of the CA- and P-codes, the GPS receiver must be in line of sight with two satellites at least 25 degrees above the horizon.

Chapter 8: Global Positioning System

MULTIPLE CHOICE QUESTIONS

name:

date:

9. The basic GPS service fails to meet four basic criteria necessary for aircraft navigation. What are these four criteria?
   a. Redundancy, reliability, accuracy and accountability
   b. Vulnerability, performance, reliability and maintainability
   c. Accuracy, availability, integrity and continuity
   d. Consistency, redundancy, integrity and accessibility

10. The Wide Area Augmentation System (WAAS) and the Local Area Augmentation System (LAAS) are both sub-categories of ____________.
    a. Course/acquisition (C/A) codes
    b. Precision (P) codes
    c. Overlay GPS
    d. Differential GPS

11. Which of the following statements is true concerning the GPS Local Area Augmentation System (LAAS)?
    a. LAAS will enhance GPS for Category II or Category III precision approaches.
    b. The next generation of GPS satellites will incorporate the LAAS enhancement.
    c. LAAS will be used primarily for enroute aircraft navigation.
    d. LAAS incorporates the use of standard VHF navigation equipment to verify GPS accuracy.

12. What TSO was approved by the FAA in 1996 to certified airborne GPS equipment for supplemental area navigation?
    a. TSO-C129a
    b. TSO-C146a
    c. TSO-C145
    d. TSC-196

13. What TSO was approved by the FAA in 2002 to certified airborne GPS equipment for "stand-alone" airborne navigation equipment using GPS/WAAS?
    a. TSO-C129a
    b. TSO-C146a
    c. TSO-C145
    d. TSC-196

14. What FAA certification standard allows airborne GPS to be used as supplemental area navigation equipment, making the monitoring of conventional navigational systems for en route and nonprecision approach navigation unnecessary?
    a. Technical standard order C129a
    b. Type certificate number C145
    c. Type certificate number C129a
    d. Technical standard order GPS145

15. What TSO was approved by the FAA in 1998 to certify airborne GPS equipment for the use with the Wide Area Augmentation System?
    a. TSO-C129a
    b. TSO-C146a
    c. TSO-C145
    d. TSC-196

16. What is the main disadvantage of portable GPS receivers for aircraft navigation?
    a. Portable GPS receivers do not meet the FAA TSO standards since they are not installed in aircraft.
    b. It is often difficult to achieve proper antenna placement for portable GPS used inside aircraft.
    c. Moving map displays are not available on portable GPS receivers.
    d. Portable GPS receivers can only track one satellite at a time and therefore respond slowly.

Chapter 8: Global Positioning System

MULTIPLE CHOICE QUESTIONS

name:

date:

17. On aircraft, many remotely mounted GPS antennas contain a signal amplifier. How is this amplifier powered?
    a. There is typically a separate circuit breaker and wiring dedicated to the antenna amplifier.
    b. The amplifier generates power from the RF signal received from the satellites.
    c. The amplifier receives power for the receiver processor through the coaxial antenna cable.
    d. The antenna contains a lithium battery, which must be tested annually and changed every five years.

18. What are the main functional areas of a typical airborne GPS receiver/processor?
    a. Each unit must contain: the L-band antenna, a spread spectrum receiver, a data processor, and an output interface.
    b. Each unit must contain: the L-band antenna, a Kalman filter, and the data processor.
    c. Each unit must contain: the L-band antenna, the Kalman filter, the data processor, and the display.
    d. Each unit must contain: the L-band antenna, the data processor, and the display.

19. What is the function of the down converter circuit found in a typical GPS receiver/processor?
    a. Filters out any extraneous signals and converts the RF input to an intermediate frequency.
    b. Provides the master time pulse for all reference frequencies within the receiver/processor.
    c. Calculates all range data using the CA- and P-code data.
    d. Converts checklist information and download the data into the GPS processor.

20. What is the function of the Kalman filter?
    a. The Kalman filter is a software algorithm used by the GPS receiver/processor during calculation of aircraft position data.
    b. The Kalman filter is contained in the GPS receiver antenna to eliminate unwanted UHF frequencies.
    c. The Kalman filter is part of the satellite software used to eliminate Ephemeris errors.
    d. The Kalman filter eliminates interference in the aircraft GPS antenna system and is only used if the antenna is mounted more than two feet from the receiver/processor.

21. Which of the following statements best describes the Allied Signal KLN90?
    a. The KLN90 is a combined VHF nav/com and GPS receiver found on many light aircraft.
    b. The KLN90 is a hand held GPS receiver with TSO C129a specifications.
    c. The KLN90 is a panel mounted GPS receiver with a moving map display found on transport category aircraft.
    d. The KLN90 is a panel mounted GPS receiver that can be found on many corporate type aircraft.

22. What is the function of the GPS-101 manufactured by IFR Systems Incorporated?
    a. The GPS–101 is a GPS simulator that is used to test aircraft GPS equipment.
    b. The GPS-101 is a handheld GPS receiver.
    c. The GPS-101 is a typical panel mounted GPS receiver/processor.
    d. The GPS-101 is a software package used to update the extended database on aircraft GPS equipment.

23. Which common aircraft radio is most likely to create interference for the GPS receiver/processor?
    a. The VHF navigation receiver
    b. The VHF communications receiver/transmitter
    c. The radar receiver/transmitter
    d. The radio altimeter receiver/transmitter

Chapter 8: Global Positioning System

ANALYSIS QUESTIONS

name:

date:

1. GPS satellites transmit information in a digital format. As seen in the following figure, the digital modulation of the carrier is achieved by shifting the phase of the carrier wave to represent a change in digital information. What is this type of modulation called: amplitude modulation, digital modulation, pseudomodulation, or phase modulation?

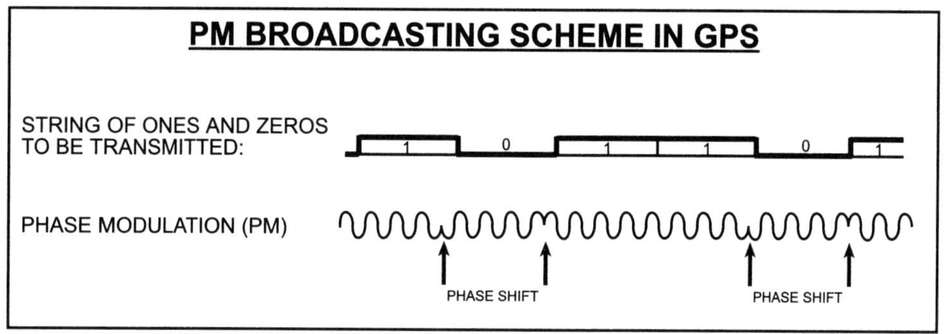

2. There are several types of errors inherent in GPS. To calculate aircraft position the receiver/ processor must compensate for these errors. The following diagram shows an aircraft location established by three GPS satellites. In this diagram, what is represented by the dotted lines: Pseudorange, TOA error, TOA range, Ephemeris range?

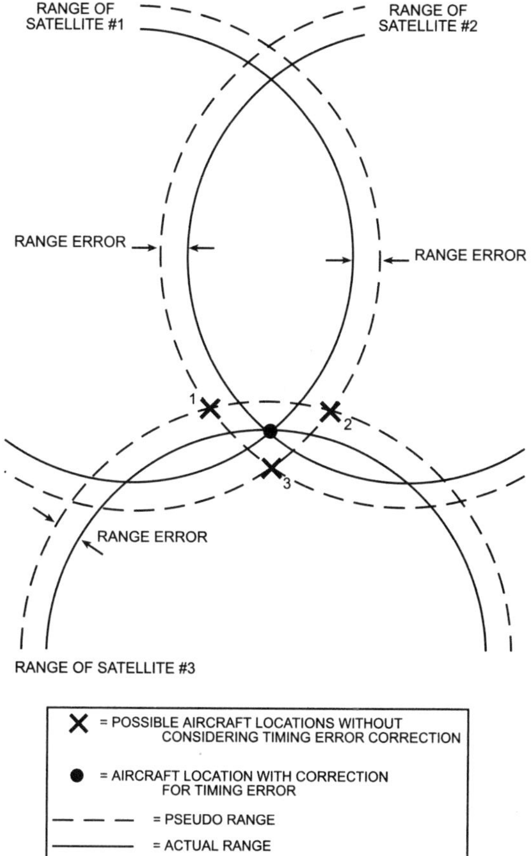

Chapter 8: Global Positioning System

ANALYSIS QUESTIONS

name:

date:

3. The basic global positioning system has several limitations that make it undesirable for aircraft navigation. Various systems are designed to increase the accuracy, availability, integrity and continuity of the basic GPS to a level sufficient for complete aircraft navigation. Which GPS enhancement does the following diagram represent: local area augmentation system, geostationary augmentation system, earth-based augmentation system, or wide area augmentation system?

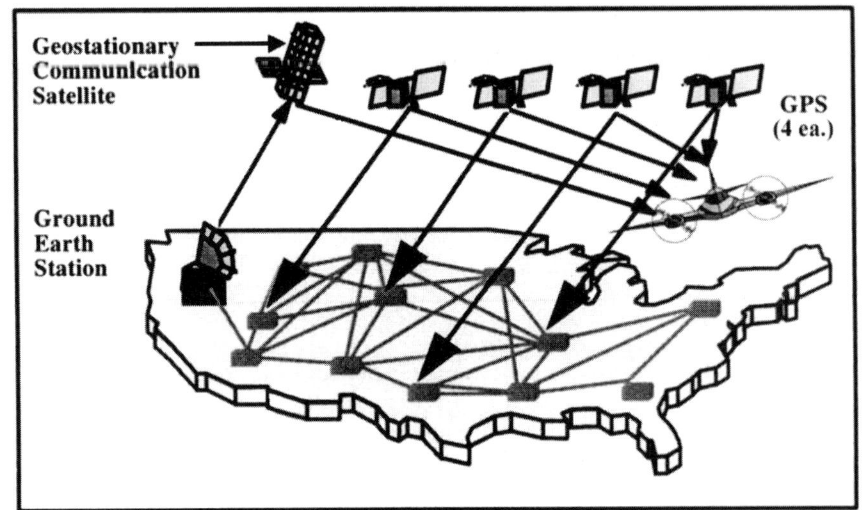

ANALYSIS QUESTIONS

name:

date:

4. In general, all civilian GPS receivers/processors contain at least four functional areas: (1) an output interface, (2) a data processor (plus software), (3) a spread spectrum receiver, and (4) the L-band antenna. In the table below, identify these four functional areas according to the following diagram.

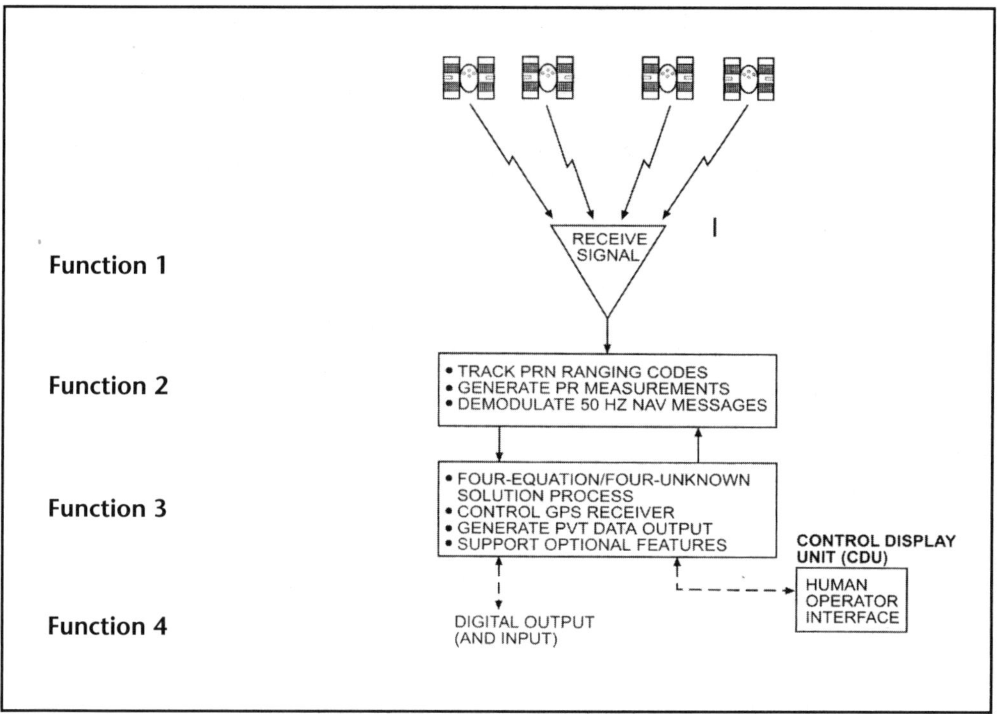

FUNCTION NUMBER	NAME OF FUNCTIONAL BLOCK
1	
2	
3	
4	

Chapter 8: Global Positioning System

ANALYSIS QUESTIONS

name:

date:

5. The block diagram of a typical five-channel GPS receiver is shown in the following diagram. Complete the table to identify the circuits and/or signals within the receiver.

   Choose from the following:

   IF signal (L_1)
   IF signal (L_2)
   quartz clock
   frequency synthesizer.

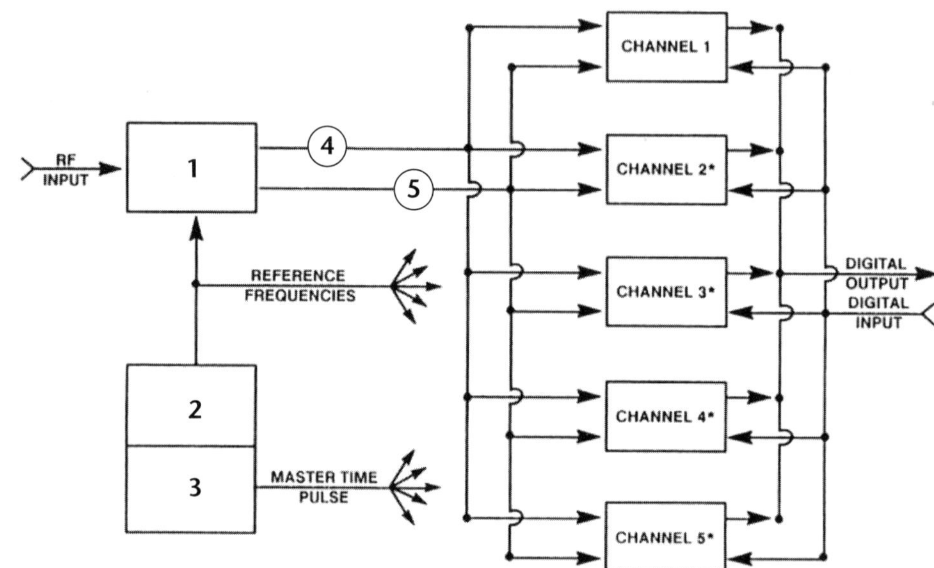

DIAGRAM NUMBER	NAME OF CIRCUIT/SIGNALS
1	
2	
3	
4	
5	

Corrections, Suggestions for Improvement, Request for Additional Information

It is Avotek's goal to provide quality aviation maintenance resources to help you succeed in your career, and we appreciate your assistance in helping.

Please complete the following information to report a correction, suggestion for improvement, or to request additional information.

REFERENCE NUMBER (*To be assigned by Avotek*)		
CONTACT INFORMATION*		
Date		
Name		
Email		
Daytime Phone		
BOOK INFORMATION		
Title		
Edition		
Page number		
Figure/Table Number		
Discrepancy/Correction (*You may also attach a copy of the discrepancy/correction*)		
Suggestion(s) for Improvement (*Attach additional documentation as needed*)		
Request for Additional Information		
FOR AVOTEK USE ONLY	Date Received	
	Reference Number Issued By	
	Receipt Notification Sent	
	Action Taken/By	
	Completed Notification Sent	

**Contact information will only be used to provide updates to your submission or if there is a question regarding your submission.*

Send your corrections to:

Email: comments@avotek.com

Fax: 1-540-234-9399

Mail: Corrections: Avotek Information Resources
P.O. Box 219
Weyers Cave, VA 24486 USA